Library of Congress Cataloging-in-Publication Data
Names: Foster, Jeff, 1971- author. | McLaughlin, Julie, 1984- illustrator.
Title: For which we stand : how our government works and why it matters / by Jeff Foster; illustrated by Julie McLaughlin.
Description: [First edition] | New York : Scholastic Inc., 2020. | Includes index. | Audience: Ages 8-12. | Summary: "Now more
than ever, it's so important for everyone to understand our government: where it came from, how it works, and how we can
bring about change. And, after all, in the words of author and government teacher Jeff Foster, 'If you don't participate, you can't
complain.' This book is a comprehensive and entertaining guide that answers questions like: What is the Constitution? What
are the branches of the government? What is the Electoral College? What are the political parties? What are the different
responsibilities of the city, state, and federal governments? Plus, discover the complete backstory on some of our government's
most important moments, like why we wrote the Declaration of Independence, and how people since then have worked with—
and protested against—the government to improve the lives of all Americans" —Provided by publisher.
Identifiers: LCCN 2020009912 | ISBN 9781338643084 (paperback) | ISBN 9781338643091 (hardcover) |
ISBN 9781338675849 (ebook)
Subjects: LCSH: United States—Politics and government—Juvenile literature. | United States—Politics and government—
History—Juvenile literature.
Classification: LCC JK40 .F67 2020 | DDC 320.473—dc23
LC record available at https://lccn.loc.gov/2020009912

10 9 8 7 6 5 4 3 2 1   20 21 22 23 24

Printed in the U.S.A.   44

First printing, September 2020

Photos ©: 47: Maurice Savage/Alamy Images; 55: Gene J. Puskar/AP Images; 61: PhotoQuest/Getty Images;
66: AP Images; 67: Rodriguez/TNS/Newscom; 91 left: UPI/Alamy Stock Photo; 91 right: Stan Honda/Getty Images;
92: Pat Benic/UPI/Newscom; 93: Harris & Ewing/Library of Congress/Corbis/VCG/Getty Images;
95: Peter Lennihan/AP Images; 105: Jonathan Ernst/Reuters/Newscom; 117: Jim West/Alamy Images;
119: Maia Kennedy/Alamy Images; 124: Mandel Ngan/Getty Images; 127: National Archives;
131: Maria Belen Perez Gabilondo/Getty Images.

All other photos © Shutterstock.com.

Illustrated by Julie McLaughlin
Book design by Heather Daugherty

To Lilly, Lucy, and the next generation of changemakers. I can't wait to see the difference that you make in the world.

—J.F.

For Which We Stand

How Our Government Works and Why It Matters

Written by Jeff Foster

Illustrated by Julie McLaughlin

Scholastic Inc.

CONTENTS

Look for highlighted glossary words throughout this book to look up more info!

YOLANDA RENEE KING

My name is Yolanda Renee King. I am eleven years old, and I am an activist, just like my grandparents, Martin Luther King, Jr. and Coretta Scott King.

I am really excited about **For Which We Stand**. Jeff Foster has been teaching so many kids for so many years about how the government works and what our rights are as citizens.

My grandparents helped to change the country—and the world—by standing up and speaking out against injustice and inequality. Because of them, I know just how important it is to understand our nation's history and how we can use that information to make America the best place it can be for all people.

My grandparents and all the people who protested with them have inspired me to get involved. I give speeches at marches and other events, and I'm passionate about issues like homelessness, protecting the environment, and stopping gun violence.

And I know that just because I'm a kid, it doesn't mean I can't make a difference in my community. There is always something we can do to work on a problem, no matter how big or small. And understanding our government and the role we play in it is an important first step to changing the world.

When I give speeches, I always end with a special chant. I ask people to repeat the words after me. It goes like this:

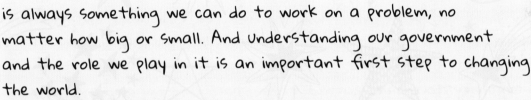

"Spread the word! Have you heard? All across the nation, we are going to be a great generation!"

I hope this book helps you learn more about the government and how we can all be more involved citizens. Together, we can change the world.

Yolanda Renee King

MY NAME IS JEFF FOSTER

and I am a teacher at Marjory Stoneman Douglas High School in Parkland, Florida. Over the last twenty years, I've taught my students how the government works and encouraged them to use their voices to make a difference. It's been an honor to see them in action, helping to pass laws that will make the world a safer place to live. But my most important job is as a parent, teaching my own daughters, Lilly and Lucy, how the government works. They are the number one reason I am writing this book.

The more you learn about how things work, the more you can use the system to help make things better. That's why I love teaching government. I try to pass along to my students everything that I've learned from books and my own experiences. I want everyone to understand that there are countless ways you can get involved and that you're never too small to make a big difference in your community.

I am lucky to live where I do. I love the United States of America, and I have always been excited by the freedoms I have as an American citizen. I love that I get to wake up every day and decide what religion I am going to practice, what kind of books that I want to read, and who I will spend my free time with.

A lot of people who live in other countries don't have the opportunity to make these kinds of choices. They might live in places with different laws that don't give them the same liberties. But we have a democracy in the United States, and this book will teach you how you can participate in that democracy to make your life—and the lives of other Americans—even better.

We are going to see how our country chooses our leaders—from the mayor of your hometown to the person who lives in the White House. You will learn how our nation started, how it has changed over the years, and how you can make it work for you. You will discover the history of America's democracy from the founding fathers (like George Washington) to current trailblazers (like Emma González). And you will realize that you're never too young or too old to make a difference.

The government is created by the people, for the people. It has been in place for more than 240 years, and we, as a society, have to continue standing up for our democracy, and for ourselves.

I can't promise that you'll ever become president of the United States, but this book will definitely help you become a better citizen. And that's even more important.

So let's get started—all you have to do now is turn the page.

wHAT IS GOVERNMENT ANYWAY?

People are always talking about how important it is to vote. But why? Does one person really make a difference?

The short answer is **YES**. In the United States, we get to decide who represents us in the government, and those people decide what rules and regulations we will have to follow. It is our responsibility to stay informed so we can shape our nation into one that provides the most good for the most people.

The role of government is to make sure society runs smoothly and that the people who live within it are safe. Without our government, we wouldn't have laws, public schools, police officers, roads, or money. We wouldn't even have a country.

But how a government exercises its power over a society depends on the form of government that is in place. Some of the different types of governments include **democracies**, **monarchies**, and **dictatorships**.

TYPES OF GOVERNMENT

Let's take a more in-depth look at different kinds of government around the world.

DEMOCRACY is government by the people. A direct democracy is when every person contributes to every decision made by the government. Some countries, like the United States, are too large for every person to be so involved. That's why the founding fathers decided to make us a representative democracy called a republic.

A republic is a form of government in which citizens elect other people to represent them in the government's decision-making. This makes it extremely important to elect representatives who will make decisions that benefit the most people.

As citizens, it is our responsibility to pay attention to what our elected officials are doing and hold them accountable for their actions. If our chosen representatives do not perform well, then it is our duty to vote them out of office during the next election.

MONARCHY is a form of government with a king or queen as the head of government. In a constitutional monarchy, the monarch's power is limited by the country's constitution. The monarch serves more of a ceremonial role, while the government is run by elected officials. However, in an absolute monarchy, the monarch has unlimited power, and he or she makes all of the governmental decisions for the country.

A **DICTATORSHIP** is an authoritarian form of government. It is known for having a single leader or group of leaders that have full authority over all decisions made by the government. The people have very little opportunity to participate in this kind of government.

Another form of authoritarian government is **FASCISM**. A fascist government is a centralized government headed by a dictator. Fascists are against democracy. They put the nation, and often race, above the individual rights of their citizens. Anyone who disagrees with the government is seen as an enemy.

COMMUNISM is a type of government in which individual people do not own land, factories, or machinery. Instead, the state owns these things. Everyone is supposed to share the wealth that they create. In a communist society, the government provides the needs of the people, including things like food, housing, and even clothing.

SOCIALISM is a type of government where there is very little private property. The government provides most necessities for its citizens, and everyone should have an equal share. Socialism is founded on the idea that people should be rewarded or paid based on the level of their individual contribution to the economy. Therefore, qualities like hard work and innovation are often valued by socialists.

THE UNITED STATES GOVERNMENT

Don't forget Alaska & Hawaii!

When the United States was founded in the late 1700s, the founding fathers had to figure out which type of government would work best for our new country. We had declared our independence from an oppressive monarchy, so everyone agreed our new government should let the people have a say in how the country was run.

They decided we would be a republic—but that was just the beginning. Then, the founding fathers had to decide how the larger federal government would work with the smaller state governments. They chose a system referred to as **federalism**. In this system, the national and the state governments share power over the people.

Federalism was Chosen For a Few Reasons:

1. It prevents any one level of government from having too much power. The federal government has specific powers granted to it by the Constitution, like declaring war, creating a national currency, and regulating trade. But according to the Tenth Amendment, any power that is not given directly to the federal government or otherwise prohibited is given to the states. The state and federal governments also share some powers, like making laws and collecting taxes.

2. It encourages political participation by the people. Any citizen can participate at any level of government. You can attend a school board meeting, have a town hall with the city mayor, protest at your state capitol, or write to your US senator. Federalism allows citizens to actively engage at all levels of government.

3. It encourages the government to be creative when trying new policies. The national government can experiment and continuously change things at the state level of government until it is effective. It can also take policies or systems that are working at the state level and expand them to the federal level. An example of this would be lowering the voting age to eighteen years old. Georgia lowered its voting age to eighteen in 1943, and a few other states soon followed. The federal government saw that its citizens supported this change, so it passed the Twenty-sixth Amendment in 1971, which lowered the voting age to eighteen in all fifty states.

FOUNDING DOCUMENTS

Some of the first and most important steps that the United States took to become its own country involved writing stuff down. First, we broke away from England with the **DECLARATION OF INDEPENDENCE**. Later, we created **THE CONSTITUTION** to serve as the basis for our new government. Now, years later, we're still writing down our most important rules and the rights of our citizens.

But, after more than 240 years, the Declaration of Independence and the US Constitution are still the two documents with the greatest impact on our society. The Declaration of Independence announced our split from England and established our "unalienable rights." Later, the Constitution defined our style of government and which of our rights are protected from government interference. These documents illustrate the philosophical and political foundations on which the founding fathers built our nation, and they are just as meaningful now as they were when they were written.

DECLARATION OF INDEPENDENCE

The Declaration of Independence was written primarily by Thomas Jefferson, and it was approved by the Continental Congress on July 4, 1776. The purpose of the Declaration of Independence was to explain why the thirteen British colonies were seeking to start their own country.

The Declaration states what rights the colonies wanted. These included the rights to life, liberty, and the pursuit of happiness. This document stated that when a government fails to protect those "unalienable rights," it is the duty of the people to overthrow that government.

Thomas Jefferson

THE DECLARATION ALSO LISTED THE 27 GRIEVANCES (OR PROBLEMS) THAT THE COLONIES HAD WITH KING GEORGE III OF ENGLAND. A FEW OF THEM WERE:

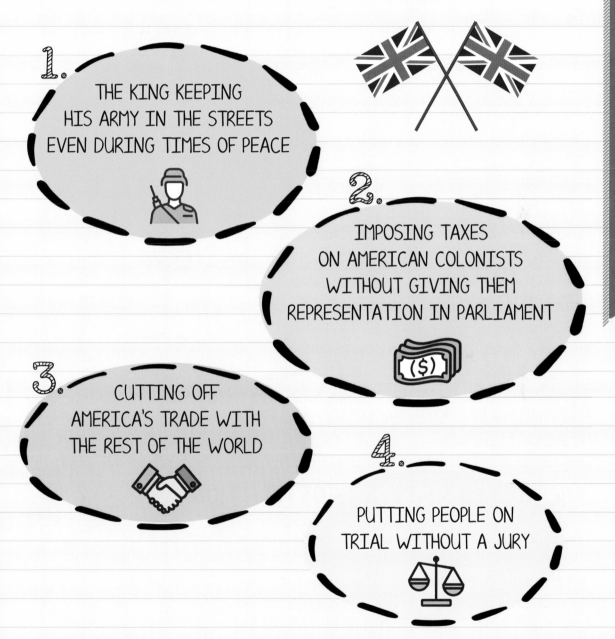

1. THE KING KEEPING HIS ARMY IN THE STREETS EVEN DURING TIMES OF PEACE

2. IMPOSING TAXES ON AMERICAN COLONISTS WITHOUT GIVING THEM REPRESENTATION IN PARLIAMENT

3. CUTTING OFF AMERICA'S TRADE WITH THE REST OF THE WORLD

4. PUTTING PEOPLE ON TRIAL WITHOUT A JURY

ARTICLES OF CONFEDERATION

During the Revolutionary War, the **THIRTEEN COLONIES** needed a way to work together to manage the war effort, conduct relations with foreign nations, and address territorial issues throughout the colonies. So they created a "league of friendship" called the **ARTICLES OF CONFEDERATION**. This governing document of the new United States was ratified by the thirteen colonies in 1781.

The Articles worked for a while, but they weren't perfect. The major downfall of the Articles of Confederation was that the document wasn't strong enough. The new federal government was too weak to enforce the Articles' laws, and therefore it had no power.

Under the Articles of Confederation, the federal government had no executive branch and no judicial branch. It couldn't raise an army or tax its citizens, and all changes to the Articles had to be agreed on by everyone. On top of that, the Continental Congress had borrowed funds to fight the Revolutionary War, and without a federal tax to raise money, the new United States could not repay its debts. A small farmers' rebellion, led by Daniel Shays in 1786-1787, showed just how weak the Articles were. This led to the need for a new government—and to the writing of the United States Constitution.

THE UNITED STATES CONSTITUTION

The Constitution is the supreme law of the United States of America. The Constitution is divided into seven articles that establish the framework of our national government. The Constitution was originally written in 1789, but since then, updates have been made to address new needs of our changing nation. These updates came in the form of the Constitution's twenty-seven amendments.

The Constitution has remained in effect because the writers did a great job of not giving too much power to any branch, level, or person within the government. Because of this, we have had the same governing document for more than two hundred years. The United States Constitution was the first document of its kind. It even inspired other nations to create their own constitutions.

SO WHAT EXACTLY IS IN OUR CONSTITUTION?

Article I created the legislative branch. It was intended to be the most powerful branch, and it takes up more than half of the words in the Constitution. It defines the structure and the powers of this part of the government.

Article II created the executive branch. The executive branch was given fewer powers than the legislative branch, because the founding fathers were afraid of creating a person who would be as powerful as a king. This article also created the Electoral College as protection against the citizens choosing an unqualified president.

Article III of the United States Constitution establishes the judicial branch of the federal government. This includes both the Supreme Court and any lower courts created by Congress. Article III defines **treason** and allows the courts to handle cases or controversies arising under federal law.

Article IV defines interstate relations, or the relationships between the states. It includes clauses that allow contracts in one state, like drivers' licenses, to be valid in another state (full faith and credit clause); protections against discrimination from state to state (the privileges and immunities clause); and an **extradition** clause that requires fugitives to be sent back to the state from which they fled. Article IV also guarantees each state a republican form of government.

Article V describes the process of how the Constitution can be amended. It lists four total ways that the Constitution can be changed: two ways to propose a change and two ways to accept those proposals.

Read more about amending the Constitution on page 23.

Article VI contains the supremacy clause, which establishes the Constitution as the supreme law of the land. This means that states cannot pass laws that contradict the Constitution. This article also forbids a religious test as a requirement for holding a government position, and it holds the United States under the Constitution responsible for any outstanding debts under the Articles of Confederation.

Article VII states that nine of the thirteen states must ratify the Constitution for it to be a valid document. It took nearly two-and-a-half years for all thirteen states to ratify because the states refused to sign until the Bill of Rights was added to the Constitution.

HOW TO AMEND THE CONSTITUTION

Amendments can be proposed by a vote of two-thirds of the members of both chambers of Congress or a vote of two-thirds of the state legislatures, which requests Congress to call a national convention to propose amendments.

To ratify, or accept, an amendment, the Constitution allows two methods: a favorable vote in three-fourths of the state legislatures or a favorable vote in specially called ratifying conventions in three-fourths of the states.

Twenty-six of the twenty-seven constitutional amendments were passed with a proposal of two-thirds of the House and the Senate, which was then ratified by three-fourths of the state governments. The Twenty-first Amendment, which repealed prohibition, was proposed in the same way, but it was ratified by three-fourths of the states after a special state convention vote instead.

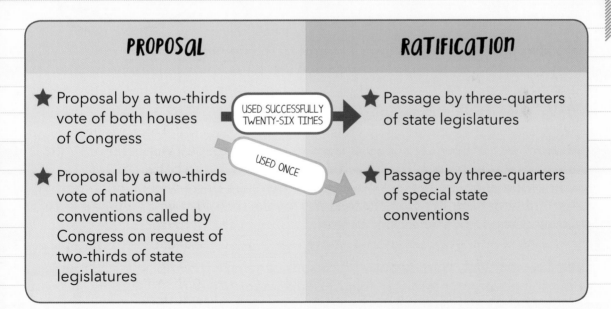

PROPOSAL	RATIFICATION
★ Proposal by a two-thirds vote of both houses of Congress	★ Passage by three-quarters of state legislatures
★ Proposal by a two-thirds vote of national conventions called by Congress on request of two-thirds of state legislatures	★ Passage by three-quarters of special state conventions

USED SUCCESSFULLY TWENTY-SIX TIMES

USED ONCE

BILL OF RIGHTS

The founding fathers knew that as time went on and our country got bigger, we would need to make changes to the Constitution in the form of amendments. The first ten amendments, known as the Bill of Rights, were added to the Constitution just two years later, in 1791. The Bill of Rights was added to offer specific protections to individuals and to place restrictions on the powers of government.

The **1ST AMENDMENT** extends the freedom of speech, religion, press, assembly, and petition to its citizens. **Speech** is fully protected as long as your words do not put others in danger. For example, you can say that you don't like or agree with the president, but you cannot yell "Bomb!" in a crowded area, which could cause chaos and injuries.

Freedom of religion prevents the government from establishing a national religion or doing anything to promote or hinder any specific religion. It also allows citizens to follow whatever religion they want.

Read more about separation of church and state on page 35.

Freedom of the press allows all forms of the media to function without government interference. That means that the press is where citizens can be exposed to a wide range of information and opinions, and where the government can be held accountable.

Freedom of assembly allows citizens to gather together publicly without interference from the government. Many of our nation's greatest accomplishments, like the civil rights movement, are protected by our freedom to assemble peacefully. Then, citizens can invoke their final First Amendment protected freedom: freedom of petition.

Freedom of petition means that citizens can make a complaint about the government without fear of punishment. We can assemble and raise awareness about an issue that we are passionate about and petition the government to make a change.

The **2ND AMENDMENT** allows citizens to bear arms. This means that citizens have the right to own and keep firearms.

The **3RD AMENDMENT** denies soldiers access to people's homes during wartime or peace without their consent.

The **4TH AMENDMENT** protects citizens against illegal searches of them or their property without reasonable suspicion.

The **5TH AMENDMENT** protects citizens from being put on trial for the same crime twice. This is called double jeopardy. It also protects you from having to testify against yourself in a trial (self-incrimination).

The **6TH AMENDMENT** grants every citizen the right to counsel (an attorney). It also guarantees everyone a fair and speedy trial if they are accused of a crime.

The **7TH AMENDMENT** allows all citizens the right to a jury trial when there is at least $20 at stake in a civil case.

The **8TH AMENDMENT** ensures that no excessive bail can be set against a defendant and no cruel or unusual punishment will be inflicted after a guilty verdict.

The **9TH AMENDMENT** states that any rights not mentioned in the Constitution are granted to the citizens. It was meant to protect citizens from an overly intrusive government. The right to privacy has been protected by this amendment.

The **10TH AMENDMENT** gives any power not specifically granted to the federal government by the Constitution to the states. These are called reserved powers. For example, education is not mentioned in the Constitution, which allows the states to control education policies.

Read more about the role of state governments on page 46.

OTHER CONSTITUTIONAL AMENDMENTS

The **11TH AMENDMENT** (1795) protects states from lawsuits filed by citizens of other states or from different countries.

The **12TH AMENDMENT** (1804) created separate elections for the president and vice president in the Electoral College. This changed the old rule of the candidate receiving the most votes becoming president, and the candidate with the second most votes becoming vice president.

The **13TH AMENDMENT** (1865) abolished slavery.

The **14TH AMENDMENT** (1868) is broken down into a few main clauses. The citizenship clause provides a broad definition of citizenship so that people who were formerly enslaved would be considered American citizens. The due process clause protects all citizens from having their individual liberties taken away by the government. And the equal protection clause protects citizens from discrimination based on their race, gender, sexual orientation, or religion.

The **15TH AMENDMENT** (1870) prevents the states and the federal government from denying a person the right to vote based on race, religion, or whether they had previously been enslaved. Southern states got around this amendment for many years by forcing African Americans to pass a literacy test or pay a poll tax to vote, until the Voting Rights Act put an end to these practices in 1965.

Read more about voter suppression on page 64.

The **16TH AMENDMENT** (1913) allows Congress to impose a federal income tax.

The **17TH AMENDMENT** (1913) took the power of appointing national senators from the state governments and gave it to the people of the states. After this amendment, citizens could directly elect their two senators.

The **18TH AMENDMENT** (1919) established the prohibition of "intoxicating liquors" in the United States. People in the temperance movement fought to outlaw alcohol, saying that drinking led to poverty and other issues in society.

The **19TH AMENDMENT** (1920) prevented the states or the national government from denying Americans the right to vote based on their sex. This amendment essentially extended suffrage to women.

The **20TH AMENDMENT** (1933) shortened the time from the election to the inauguration of the president and Congress. National elections are held in November, and before the Twentieth Amendment was passed, newly elected officials wouldn't start their terms until March 4 the following year. This amendment moved the congressional start date to January 3 and the presidential start date to January 20.

Read more about inauguration on page 91.

The **21ST AMENDMENT** (1933) repealed the Eighteenth Amendment, making the consumption of alcohol legal again in the United States.

THE 22ND AMENDMENT (1951) limited the president to serving two terms in office. Presidents starting with George Washington always stepped down after completing their second four-year term. This changed when the 32nd president, Franklin D. Roosevelt (FDR), was elected to four terms in office. In response to this, Congress and the states proposed and passed the Twenty-second Amendment to prevent it from happening again.

Franklin D. Roosevelt

The **23RD AMENDMENT** (1961) granted Washington, DC, three electoral votes in the presidential election.

The **24TH AMENDMENT** (1964) banned poll taxes as a requirement to vote in both state and federal elections. Poll taxes were used by southern states to try to prevent African Americans from voting.

The **25TH AMENDMENT** (1967) creates the order of succession if the president is unable to fulfill his or her duties or dies in office. The vice president and the cabinet have to formally recommend to Congress that the president cannot perform his job. The president would then have a certain amount of time to prove to Congress that he or she is capable of regaining their duties as president of the United States.

Read more about the order of succession on page 89.

The **26TH AMENDMENT** (1971) prevents the federal government from denying the vote to citizens who are at least eighteen years old. Previously, the voting age had been twenty-one years old in many states.

The **27TH AMENDMENT** (1992) prohibits any law that increases or decreases the salaries of Congress from taking effect until the next term of Congress begins.

29

WHAT DOES THE GOVERNMENT LOOK LIKE?

Since its creation, the main function of the US federal government has been creating and enforcing laws to guarantee order and consistency within our society. But the founding fathers feared any single person or branch of government having too much power. They wanted our new government to be different from the one they had left behind in England. To prevent any branch from dominating the others, the founders separated lawmaking powers among the three branches in the Constitution, each with its own specific duties and responsibilities: legislative, executive, and judicial.

The **LEGISLATIVE BRANCH**, composed of the House of Representatives and the Senate, creates laws. The **EXECUTIVE BRANCH**, led by the president, is responsible for enforcing laws. The **JUDICIAL BRANCH**, which includes a federal court system headed by the Supreme Court, decides whether these laws are in violation of the Constitution. This separation of powers prevents any one branch from gaining too much control.

THE THREE BRANCHES

1. THE LEGISLATIVE BRANCH

The **LEGISLATIVE BRANCH** is responsible for writing legislation (laws). This branch is broken up into two chambers: the House of Representatives and the Senate. In the federal government, there are **100 SENATORS** and **435 HOUSE MEMBERS**. Each of the fifty states has two senators. But the number of representatives that each state has in the House depends on its population. For instance, California has the largest population of any state, so it has the most representatives in the House (fifty-three). The seven states with the smallest populations (Alaska, Delaware, Montana, North Dakota, South Dakota, Vermont, and Wyoming) only have one representative each. Each state also has its own legislative branch as well.

Powers of the legislative branch at the national level include making laws, declaring war, regulating trade, overriding executive branch **vetoes**, charging government officials with any crimes that have been committed, collecting taxes, and raising an army.

MORE BRANCHES OF GOVT.

2. THE EXECUTIVE BRANCH

At the federal level, the **EXECUTIVE BRANCH** is made up of the president, vice president, and a collection of agencies that carry out laws. The states have a governor, lieutenant governor, and their own collection of agencies to carry out state laws.

Executive powers at both the federal and state level include signing and vetoing laws, **appointing** judges and heads of executive agencies, and **pardoning** criminals. The federal executive branch is also responsible for acting as commander in chief for the military and greeting leaders from other nations.

3. THE JUDICIAL BRANCH

The **JUDICIAL BRANCH** was created to help interpret the laws that the other branches write and enforce. This collection of judges acts like a referee and gets to decide whether what is being done by the legislative and executive branches is legal.

CHECKS AND BALANCES

The founding fathers wanted to ensure that no one branch would have too much power, so they created a system of checks and balances within the three branches.

LEGISLATIVE

CHECKS ON:

EXECUTIVE	JUDICIAL
★ The Senate confirms presidential appointments.	★ The Senate confirms judges.
★ Congress can override a veto with a two-thirds vote in both the House and the Senate.	★ Congress can change the number of judges that sit on the Supreme Court.
★ Congress can impeach and remove the president.	★ Congress can also revise legislation or pass a constitutional amendment when one of their laws is ruled unconstitutional by the courts.
★ The Senate ratifies treaties made by the president.	★ Congress can also impeach and remove judges.

33

EXECUTIVE

CHECKS ON:

LEGISLATIVE	JUDICIAL
★ The president can veto a law.	★ The president appoints all federal judges.
★ The executive branch does not have to enforce a law passed by Congress.	★ The executive branch does not have to enforce judicial decisions.
	★ Presidents and governors can pardon people convicted of crimes by the court system.

JUDICIAL

CHECKS ON:

LEGISLATIVE	EXECUTIVE
★ The courts can rule laws unconstitutional.	★ The courts can rule executive actions unconstitutional.

CHURCH and STATE

There are other systems of separation in the Constitution, too, like that of church and state. The founders wanted to ensure that government and religion would remain separate. The clause dealing with religion in the First Amendment states that "Congress shall make no law respecting an establishment of religion, or prohibiting the free exercise thereof."

The first part **(THE ESTABLISHMENT CLAUSE)** ensures that no government in the US will openly support a specific religion. So any time that a law is written to help or hurt a religion, the courts are supposed to rule the law **unconstitutional** so it doesn't violate the First Amendment.

The second part **(THE FREE EXERCISE CLAUSE)** means that the government cannot prevent any individual from believing in whatever religion they choose. However, the practice of religion is not fully protected by the Constitution. Those who break the law in the name of religion can still be arrested.

35

POLITICAL PARTIES

Most times when people have the ability to decide something for a larger group of people, opposing sides form. People who agree about a certain idea join together to increase their power and try to get as many people as possible to join their side. This is how political parties began.

The goal of any political party in the United States is to win the majority of the seats in one or both of the chambers of Congress. This allows that party to control what laws get introduced and passed in the country until the next election. The best way for a political party to do this is to try to appeal to many different kinds of voters. That's why a two-party system has developed in America. The more groups that a party can appeal to, the more likely they are to win elections. In almost all of the elections in the United States, the candidate who has the most votes is declared the winner of the election.

THERE ARE ADVANTAGES AND DISADVANTAGES TO HAVING A TWO-PARTY SYSTEM.

On the **PLUS SIDE**, the government is more stable and is able to run more smoothly with only two parties. Both parties are used to dealing with each other, and they understand the goals of the other, despite their differences. And since neither party wants to lose voters in future elections, they make only minor changes when they gain control, rather than radically changing the government. That's why these two parties have controlled the government for almost a century.

Hey, not bad!

The **BAD PART** of a two-party system is that citizens are left with fewer choices. They may end up siding with the party they disagree with the *least*, rather than one they feel strongly about. Voters might even stop participating in government because of their lack of options or think their vote doesn't matter as much. A two-party system also makes it difficult for third parties to introduce new ideas, since voters know third-party candidates are less likely to be elected.

Room for improvement!

The modern two-party system in America is dominated by the Democratic Party and the Republican Party. One of these two parties has won every United States presidential election since 1852 and has held the majority in the United States Congress since 1856.

The **DEMOCRATIC PARTY** was founded in 1828. Today, the party is generally associated with:

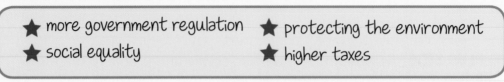

- ★ more government regulation
- ★ social equality
- ★ protecting the environment
- ★ higher taxes

Members of the Democratic Party are often referred to as "progressives" or "liberals." The symbol of the Democratic Party is a donkey.

The Democratic Party evolved from the Democratic-Republican Party, which was founded in 1792 by Thomas Jefferson, James Madison, and other prominent opponents of the Federalists. But the modern Democratic Party actually began in the 1830s with the election of Andrew Jackson. Known as the party of the "common man," the early Democratic Party stood for individual rights and state **sovereignty** and opposed banks and the abolition of slavery.

Alexander Hamilton

FACT

The Federalists were the first political party in the United States. They were supporters of the Constitution and a strong central government. Famous Federalists included Alexander Hamilton and President John Adams.

The **REPUBLICAN PARTY** was founded in 1854 by antislavery activists. Today, the party is generally associated with:

★ a strong national defense

★ little government interference in economic policy

★ more government interference in social policies

Members of the Republican Party are often referred to as "conservatives," and the party symbol is an elephant. The early Republican Party consisted of factory workers, farmers, businessmen and professionals, African Americans, and northern white Protestants.

Both the Republican and Democratic parties have changed dramatically since their early years, much like the country itself. The two parties have essentially swapped their primary causes and supporters since they were first founded in the mid-1800s. The Democratic Party of today supports minority rights, the environment, and heavier regulation of businesses. Meanwhile, today's Republican Party is one that favors a strong national defense, lower taxes for businesses and the wealthy, protection of gun rights, and fewer restrictions on businesses.

As time marches on, it will be interesting to see how the Democratic and Republican parties continue to evolve and whether or not the American two-party system will endure.

THIRD PARTIES

Third parties have come and gone in American politics. Most third-party candidates fizzle out very quickly, since many voters do not want to waste their vote on a candidate that they don't think will win against their Democratic or Republican opponents.

However, there have been some third parties throughout the years that have had a substantial following and impacted several elections. This usually occurs when a third-party candidate takes votes from one of the two major parties. In a close election, a third-party candidate can cost one of their opponents the presidency!

The **WHIG PARTY** operated from approximately 1832 to 1856. The Whigs were created to oppose the policies of President Andrew Jackson and the Democratic Party. The party believed that the legislative branch should have more power than the executive branch and that it was the government's duty to assist in economic development. Four presidents were elected under the banner of the Whig Party.

The **PROGRESSIVE PARTY**, also known as the Bull Moose Party, was a short-lived third party in the United States. It was formed in 1912 by former president Theodore Roosevelt after he lost the Republican Party presidential nomination to his conservative rival, incumbent president William Howard Taft. This party was known for supporting new ideas that would drastically change the political system. The Progressives supported the idea of women's suffrage; a shorter, eight-hour workday; and having the people directly elect their senators.

Theodore Roosevelt

The **GREEN PARTY** is a political party based on the principles of green politics, such as environmentalism, nonviolence, and social justice. Members of this party believe that advocating for these issues can lead to a more peaceful world. The party has existed in the United States since 1984.

Businessman Ross Perot founded the **REFORM PARTY** in 1995 after claiming that Americans were disillusioned with the existing two-party system. The Reform party was meant to be an alternative to the Republican and Democratic beliefs about what the government should be allowed to do and how much interference it should have in its citizens' lives.

The **TEA PARTY** (which some say stands for "taxed enough already") is a conservative political movement within the Republican Party. The party was created in 2009 in response to the economic policies of President Obama. Members of the Tea Party have demanded lower taxes and the need for a balanced budget to reduce the national debt.

In 1992, President George H. W. Bush lost the election for a second term. Third-party candidate Ross Perot received votes from many people who normally voted Republican, which may have contributed to Bush's loss. His son President George W. Bush also had a close election in 2000. His election win may have been partly because many voters chose third-party candidate Ralph Nader instead of the Democratic candidate, Al Gore. Nader's votes may have cost Bush's opponent a chance to win close states (particularly Flordia) that cost Gore the Electoral College.

Read more about the Electoral College on page 73.

41

HOW DOES THE GOVERNMENT WORK IN MY COMMUNITY?

When most people think about the government, they think about Washington, DC. But there are smaller forms of government in every city and state in the country! That's because our country is too big to let just one group be responsible for everything. So the federal government shares its job with the governments of each state.

Here's how some of the biggest tasks are split up to keep our country running.

STATE RESPONSIBILITIES

★ Plan roads

★ Run public schools

★ Provide water

★ Organize police and fire services

★ License professions such as teachers and lawyers

★ Arrange elections for the people

FEDERAL RESPONSIBILITIES

★ Declare war

★ Run postal services

★ Regulate air travel

★ Make treaties with foreign nations

★ Impose tariffs

★ Regulate trade between states

★ Coin money

Most state power comes from the Tenth Amendment to the US Constitution. Any powers not given directly to the national government by the Constitution are given to the states.

STATES HAVE USED THE TENTH AMENDMENT TO:

administer elections ★ create traffic laws ★ collect local taxes

However, the Constitution includes two clauses that have been cited by the Supreme Court over the years to expand the federal government's power. The **NECESSARY AND PROPER CLAUSE** allows Congress to do whatever it sees fit to help carry out its given Constitutional powers. An example would be when it created a national bank, which allowed it to carry out its power to collect taxes and coin money. The **SUPREMACY CLAUSE** states the Constitution is the supreme law of the land, so state laws cannot contradict federal laws.

CITY GOVERNMENT

One of the smallest forms of government is at the city level. A city government oversees the operation and functions of a city or town. It provides clean water and sewage service to the citizens of the city, and it maintains parks, streetlights, and the zoning of the city.

The **CITY COUNCIL** is elected by the people. Its members are responsible for making policies that impact the city's residents. Just like members of Congress, the city council proposes bills to discuss and vote on and passes new laws to help govern the city.

The **MAYOR** is also an elected position, and he or she is usually part of the city council, too. The mayor is responsible for hiring and firing staff and usually presides over city meetings. The mayor also performs most of the ceremonial duties of the city.

The **CITY MANAGER** manages the day-to-day operations of the city. Unlike the mayor, the city manager is not elected. This position is typically appointed by the city council. The city manager controls the budget and oversees the workers who are carrying out the daily operations of the city.

The **POLICE CHIEF** and **FIRE CHIEF** are the respective heads of the police and fire departments. Both roles can be either elected or appointed, depending on the city or county. Each chief is responsible for managing their department's budget and operations.

COUNTY GOVERNMENT

A county government is created by the state to service an area bigger than a city. Its elected officials enforce state laws, collect taxes, and record public documents. They are also responsible for assessing property, maintaining roads, and conducting elections in the county. In addition, the county government maintains parks, libraries, sewers, and emergency management for the cities under its domain.

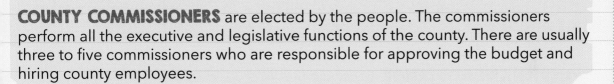

COUNTY COMMISSIONERS are elected by the people. The commissioners perform all the executive and legislative functions of the county. There are usually three to five commissioners who are responsible for approving the budget and hiring county employees.

COUNTY ENGINEERS are responsible for planning, building, and maintaining roads, canals, pipelines, and powerlines for the county.

Members of the **SCHOOL BOARD** organize schools, create boundaries, control the budget, and decide the curriculum that is followed in county public schools. (Although some school boards occur at the city level instead.)

The **COUNTY CORONER** is responsible for investigating any deaths within the county's borders.

A **SHERIFF** serves as the chief law-enforcement officer for his or her county. This is an elected position, and the sheriff's responsibilities include providing security for the county courtrooms, serving warrants, and maintaining the county's jails.

The **COUNTY AUDITOR** has oversight over all financial records for the county. Their job is to make sure that all of the county's money is spent appropriately. The auditor also has investigative authority over all money within the county.

The **COUNTY CLERK** maintains all the court records in the county. He or she is responsible for birth, death, and marriage certificates. The clerk also collects all property taxes, which fund public schools.

STATE GOVERNMENT

The state government is divided into three branches, just like the federal government. It is responsible for overseeing the daily administration of the entire state.

The **GOVERNOR** is the chief executive of the state; it is similar to being president at the state level. The governor signs statewide laws and also has power to veto them. He or she is commander in chief of the National Guard, can grant pardons to people convicted of crimes in the state, and has appointment power for state officials.

The **LIEUTENANT GOVERNOR** is the second in command in the state, similar to the vice president at the state level. He or she fills in for the governor if they are unavailable, and they often preside over the state senate. The duties of the lieutenant governor vary from state to state.

The two chambers of the **STATE LEGISLATURE** propose laws that will affect all people in the state. This process is similar to how laws are passed at the national level.

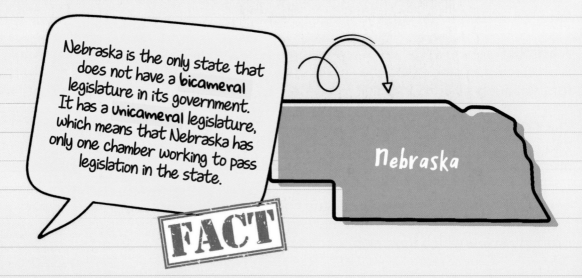

Nebraska is the only state that does not have a **bicameral** legislature in its government. It has a **unicameral** legislature, which means that Nebraska has only one chamber working to pass legislation in the state.

Nebraska

FACT

The **ATTORNEY GENERAL** is the top law-enforcement officer in the state. He or she protects the rights of the people while defending the state in legal matters. Some states appoint their attorney general, but most are elected by the people.

The **STATE AUDITOR** reviews the finances of the state government and makes sure that it has a balanced budget.

It is just as important to be involved in the government in your own community as it is to be involved at the national level. These smaller forms of government impact the place you live every day—from the roads you drive on, the water that you drink, and what you learn in school! If you want to make a difference for the people around you, sometimes your local or state government is the best place to start.

HARRISBURG, PA., CAPITOL BUILDING

HOW DO YOU RUN FOR A POLITICAL OFFICE?

There are a lot of different jobs to fill in the government, but it's not easy to get elected into those spots. First, the people who are interested have to campaign for the job—and hope that voters choose them.

STATE AND LOCAL ELECTIONS are held at different times throughout the year. State elections include races for governor, state legislature, and state supreme court. Cities and counties have elections for mayor, city commissioners, judges, and many other offices.

The United States holds **FEDERAL ELECTIONS** every two years (on even-numbered years). The people and positions that are on each ballot vary depending on who is up for reelection or whose terms in office are up.

 A presidential election is held every four years.

 House members serve two-year terms, so they are up for reelection every two years.

 Senators serve six-year terms, so one-third of the senate is up for reelection every two years.

 Senators and representatives can serve unlimited terms, but the president is limited to two terms in office.

WHY DO PEOPLE RUN FOR OFFICE?

People who run for office vary greatly in terms of their beliefs, goals, campaign strategies, and reasons for running. Most people who run for office are motivated by the fact that they can effect change within their community. **Elected officials get to turn their ideas into policies that can impact thousands of people and improve their lives.** But running for office isn't easy. It is an enormous commitment that can take lots of time, money, and hard work.

GETTING ON THE BALLOT

It costs millions of dollars to run for a spot in the US House and Senate. Most of the money for these campaigns comes from donations from individuals and interest groups.

Read more about interest groups on page 116.

Most races for the House are considered "safe seats," which means that the incumbent (the person currently in office) has a great chance of winning reelection. There are many reasons for this.

★ WHY DO INCUMBENTS USUALLY WIN REELECTION? ★

NAME RECOGNITION

Most voters tend to vote for someone whose name they have seen before. Since the incumbent has likely been in the news during their term, they generally have more name recognition than their opponent.

EASIER TO RAISE MONEY

Donors are much more likely to donate their money to the person currently holding office, since they have a better chance of winning. Supporting an incumbent may also give the donor access to that candidate once they are reelected.

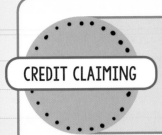

CREDIT CLAIMING

Whether taking credit for a good economy or helping with a relief effort after a natural disaster, elected officials always take credit for anything positive that happened to his or her constituents during their time in office.

GERRYMANDERING

A large number of congressional districts are drawn in a way that favors the controlling party, which makes it nearly impossible for the incumbent's opponent to win.

Read more about gerrymandering on page 66.

The incumbency rate (the percentage of times that a person in office wins reelection) in the House of Representatives is more than 90 percent. The incumbency rate in the Senate is between 80 and 90 percent.

A challenger is slightly more likely to win against an incumbent in the Senate than in the House. This is because the challengers are often more well-known. People often run for the Senate after serving as governor or in the House of Representatives, so they already have name recognition. Senate candidates also have to appeal to a more diverse population, not just the people of one district, and they must have a more general platform that appeals to the entire state.

STEP-BY-STEP CAMPAIGNING

Candidates who run for a **HOUSE OR A SENATE SEAT** follow a similar path when trying to get elected.

STEP 1

First, they must officially announce their candidacy and file the proper paperwork to get on the ballot.

STEP 2

Then there's a primary election in which the candidates from the same party run against each other.

STEP 3

The winners of the Democratic and Republican primary elections then compete against each other in the general election to determine who will win the Congressional seat.

There's a similar chain of events for anyone **RUNNING FOR PRESIDENT**.

STEP 1

Presidential candidates usually announce their intention to run for the White House about eighteen months before the general election.

STEP 2

Like in the congressional races, each party's candidates battle with each other to win their party's nomination.

STEP 3

The winners of the two nominations go on the official presidential ballot. The candidates who do not win usually turn their efforts to helping the chosen candidate from their party win the election.

Whether Democrat, Republican, or a third party, the goal of any candidate trying to become president is to appeal to as many groups of people as possible. America is a diverse country, and in order to do well, a candidate has to try to get as many votes as possible. This is why people running for president usually support many moderate positions.

DEBATES between the possible candidates for the Republican and Democratic nominations usually begin the summer before the primary and caucus season. In recent years, there have been upward of twenty candidates seeking the nomination from their party to run for president.

The first stage of debates is between different members of the same party. The Democratic and Republican debates serve to differentiate the candidates as they try to sell the American voters on their ideas. Since the candidates are from the same party, the tone of the debate is usually more polite and civil than it is when the two parties are debating each other.

Poll numbers determine which candidates get a preferred center spot on the stage during the debates and more air time on the news. Lesser-known candidates try to make a name for themselves by confronting the favored candidates on the stage, while the front-runners try to avoid saying things that will hurt their popularity.

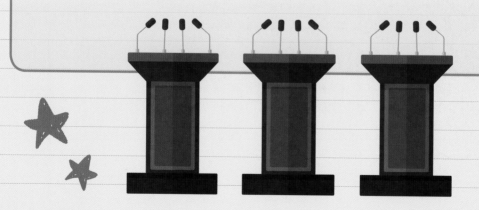

PRIMARIES AND CAUCUSES

The candidates try to gain their party's nomination by winning a combination of primaries and caucuses: two ways in which members of the parties vote for who they want to see on the presidential ticket.

PRIMARIES are much more common, and they are used by the vast majority of the fifty states. In a primary election, each voter usually gets a ballot at a polling place, and they vote for their favorite candidate among those competing in their party. The candidate who receives the most votes receives most of its delegates.

Read more about conventions on page 59.

FACT

Delegates are people who represent their state at a party convention. Candidates earn delegates' votes for winning and placing highly in primaries and caucuses in the presidential election. The candidate who receives the majority of delegates from all of the states wins the nomination from their party.

2020 IOWA CAUCUS

CAUCUSES are used in just a handful of states, including Iowa. This process is a little more complicated than voting in a primary.

1 On Election Day, the voters from each party show up at different meeting places across the state to discuss the candidates and try to convince others to support their preferred nominee. In bigger cities they often meet in high schools and auditoriums, while in smaller towns they might meet at the local fire or police station.

2 During the caucus, several rounds of voting take place. A candidate has to qualify to earn delegates by receiving a certain number of votes.

3 If a candidate receives less than 15 percent of the vote, they are eliminated from that caucus; their supporters can then change their vote to another candidate.

4 The attendees continue voting until the remaining candidates have received the minimum number of votes needed to move on.

5 The votes from all of the voting sites are then counted together, and delegates are awarded to the candidates who have qualified. Usually, multiple candidates will receive delegates from the state, but the highest vote getter is still declared the winner.

Caucuses require a lot more time from voters. It might take multiple hours to participate in a caucus, compared to just a few minutes to vote in a primary. Due to this, caucus voters tend to be better informed, and they are usually more passionate about the candidates.

FACT

To participate in most primary and caucus elections, you must be registered with one of the two political parties.

The **IOWA CAUCUS**, held in late January or early February of a presidential election year, is the first contest in the nomination calendar.

The nation's first primary takes place in **NEW HAMPSHIRE**, typically a week after the Iowa caucus. Since these states are always the first two on the nomination calendar, both party's candidates spend a lot of time campaigning there. It's very important to finish high in both states if a candidate wants to have a chance at securing the nomination.

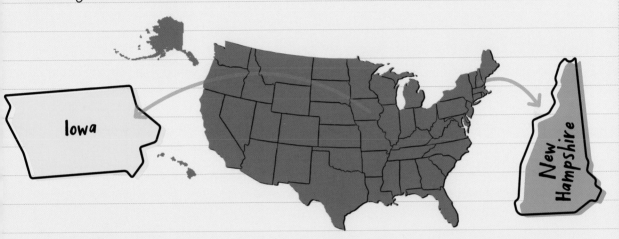

After the contests in Iowa and New Hampshire are over, the other forty-eight states, plus the US territories and Washington, DC, have their own primaries and caucuses that occur over the next six months. With each one, presidential candidates are trying to earn delegates on their way to the nomination. Those who do not perform well during this stage tend to drop out of the race and usually throw their support behind one of the remaining candidates.

One of the biggest days in the nomination calendar is called **SUPER TUESDAY**, which takes place in March. On this day, more than a dozen states—and sometimes almost double that number—hold their primaries and caucuses. The winner of the majority of Super Tuesday states often ends up winning the nomination for their party.

Their running mate, the candidate for vice president, is usually selected later in the summer by the presidential candidate and other members from their party.

THE PRESIDENTIAL CANDIDATE USUALLY CHOOSES SOMEONE FOR VICE PRESIDENT WHO HELPS BALANCE THE TICKET FOR VARIOUS REASONS.

He or she might be chosen to appeal to a different part of the country. For instance, if the presidential nominee is from the South, a vice president might be chosen from the Northeast, Midwest, or West Coast.

The VP might also be chosen from a state that is important to winning the election, like the governor from Florida or a congressperson from Pennsylvania or Ohio.

Ohio

Sometimes, if the presidential nominee seems inexperienced, the vice president will be someone who has been in politics for a long time who can help the president and ease voters' concerns.

Other times, the vice president might be someone who appeals to a different group of voters. For example, if the presidential candidate is more extreme politically, the VP might be chosen because he or she has a more moderate ideology (or vice versa).

Overall, the vice president is chosen to try to get as many extra votes as possible.

VOTE

DeMOCRATIC AND REPUBLICAN CONVENTIONS

After all the states have completed their elections and the primary winners have been declared, the presidential and vice presidential candidates for each party are made official at the nominating **conventions**.

The convention is a four-day pep rally, usually held in July or August of a presidential election year. The party that the current president belongs to has their convention the week after the challenging party has theirs.

The conventions present many different speakers to showcase all the different ideas within the party and to try to appeal to as many groups of people as possible. The first and second nights of the convention are both highlighted by a keynote speaker.

The keynote speakers are either celebrities who support the candidate, former presidents, family members, or other powerful politicians—past and present—from that party.

BARACK OBAMA gained fame when he delivered the keynote address at the Democratic National Convention (DNC) in 2004. Four short years later, he was accepting the Democratic nomination for president.

On the third night of the convention, there is a roll call of the states, and they officially count the votes that were cast during the nomination season. Once a nominee receives the majority of the votes that are needed, he or she is officially nominated by the party to be their candidate in the upcoming presidential election. Later during the third night, the vice presidential candidate speaks and accepts his or her nomination.

On the last night of the convention, the presidential candidate accepts his or her nomination and gives their first speech to the American people as they strive to become the next president of the United States.

PRESIDENTIAL DEBATES

Once the party conventions are over, the presidential and vice presidential debates are scheduled. Usually, the VPs from both parties have one debate, but it doesn't have too much impact on the election.

The presidential candidates typically have three debates at three different locations, usually in swing states. The debates are often focused on different subjects, such as foreign policy, the economy, and the issues on which the candidates disagree.

Candidates spend many hours getting ready for each debate. They hold mock debates where members of their campaigns try to predict the type of questions they will get during the actual event. This allows the candidates to be better prepared and prevents them from getting surprised by any of the questions that could come up. The performance of the candidates in the debates can have a great impact on who will ultimately win the election.

In 1960, John F. Kennedy and Richard Nixon were in the first televised presidential debates in history—and one of the most famous. The election was very close, and many scholars believe that JFK gained a big edge over Nixon during the debate because he looked younger and more vibrant than Nixon, who was sweating and recovering from an injury.

HOW DOES VOTING WORK?

Once the nominees are on the ballot, the people have to decide which candidate they want to represent them in the government. It is our responsibility as citizens and as voters to determine whether our elected officials are doing what's best for their constituents.

If that answer is no, then it is our duty to vote them out of office and replace them with someone who will act with their voters' interests in mind. Whether it is reelecting someone who is already in office or voting for someone new, choosing the right people to serve in the government is one of our most important jobs as American citizens.

WHO CAN VOTE?

When the Constitution was originally written, only landowning white males were allowed to vote and be elected into offices. But since the first presidential election in 1789, amendments have been added to the Constitution that include more people in the voting process. The Fifteenth, Nineteenth, Twenty-fourth, and Twenty-sixth Amendments are all responsible for expanding suffrage, or the right to vote.

These days, to vote you **MUST BE AT LEAST 18 YEARS OLD** and a **US CITIZEN**. In in some states, you also cannot have been convicted of a felony.

Voter registration procedures vary from state to state. Some states allow people to register before they turn eighteen, some allow registration up until Election Day, and others have a registration deadline (usually around a month before the election).

FACT

National Voter Registration Day is the fourth Thursday in September.

It is important for each citizen to understand the registration process so they can participate in our government. Many high schools around the country have registration days through their social studies classes. If the schools in your area do not, maybe you can start a movement to bring registration to your school district.

VOTER SUPPRESSION

Even though there are many different ways to vote, **VOTER TURNOUT IS STILL RELATIVELY LOW** in the United States. There are many theories and explanations for why many Americans skip out on casting their ballots. But sometimes, people who want to vote aren't given the chance.

The Fifteenth Amendment, passed in 1870, was supposed to give African American men the right to vote. However, southern states found many ways to keep African Americans from participating in local and federal elections.

1. POLL TAX: African Americans were required to pay a fee (which they usually couldn't afford) in order to register to vote. This meant most African Americans were not able to take advantage of their right to vote. The Twenty-fourth Amendment, passed in 1964, outlawed all poll taxes.

2. LITERACY TESTS: When African Americans tried to register to vote, they were given a test first. These tests were filled with questions about citizenship, laws, and even logic. They were nearly impossible to pass, and most African Americans were not allowed to register to vote after failing. Literacy tests were banned with the passage of the Voting Rights Act of 1965.

3. GRANDFATHER CLAUSE: This clause stated that if your grandfather did not vote, then you were not allowed to register to vote, either. This disqualified almost every African American at the time from participating in elections. The Supreme Court ruled the grandfather clause unconstitutional in 1915.

These policies may have been eliminated, but there are still other systems in place today that make voting difficult for different parts of the population. Some states require voters to present a picture identification when voting. This makes it harder for minorities, students, and older and lower-income people to participate in elections. These groups of people are less likely to have identification cards or drivers' licenses, because it can be harder for them to get to the facilities that provide them and many do not have cars.

DRIVER LICENSE

GERRYMANDERING

But voter suppression isn't the only reason that voter turnout is low. **Many people don't show up to vote because they feel like their vote doesn't really count.** This is often the case in a district that has been **gerrymandered.**

On page 50-51, we explained that congressional incumbents usually do very well when running for reelection. One of the biggest reasons for this is tied to the concept of gerrymandering. The party in control of each state's government gets to redraw **district** lines for the House of Representatives every ten years if there is a change in the number of districts in their state.

FACT

The term "gerrymander" was coined in 1812, after Massachusetts governor Elbridge Gerry approved a redistricting bill for the state in which one redrawn district looked like a salamander.

2011 Pennslyvania Congressional Map

(with gerrymandered districts)

The districts are based on the latest census, which is the official count of the number of people living in the United States. A new census is taken every decade. The total number of citizens is then divided by 435 (the number of seats in the House of Representatives), and then the seats are redistributed among the fifty states. Any state that is given either additional or fewer seats must be redrawn.

When the seats are redrawn, the controlling party in the state legislature tends to draw them to favor their own political party, thus making it much more difficult for the opposing party to win House seats. The state legislature knows where voters live based on voter registration logs, so they can purposefully exclude certain neighborhoods in a district to guarantee their own victory. This technique essentially rigs the election in favor of one party. Because of this, there were forty-three uncontested seats in the 2018 midterm election, and only around seventy seats out of 435 were actually considered competitive.

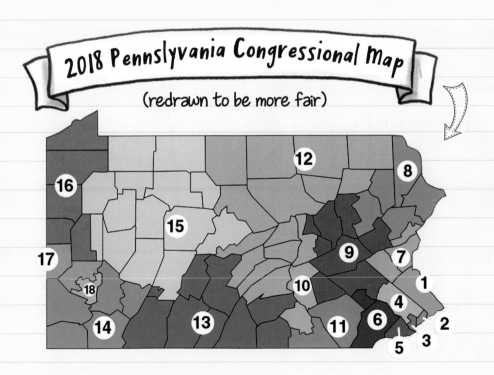

2018 Pennslyvania Congressional Map

(redrawn to be more fair)

DIFFERENT WAYS TO CAST YOUR VOTE

The presidential election is held every four years on the Tuesday after the first Monday in November. Every state—and a lot of times, every county—gets to decide how their election is conducted. These decisions include when and where the election is, how the ballot looks, and what type of ballot they are using, either paper or electronic.

Many states have instituted early voting in the last decade to make it easier for citizens to vote. Centrally located polling places are open for up to about six weeks before Election Day, and some are even open on weekends. You can also file an **absentee ballot** by mailing it in before Election Day.

A person may not display campaign material, post signs, or try to persuade a voter in any way within a polling place, within a specified distance of a building housing a polling place, or anywhere on the public property where a polling place is located, on primary or election day.

FACT

But the busiest time for voting is still on the actual day of the election. Most polls open at 7:00 am and close at 7:00 pm, but in some places they open even earlier and stay open even later. But as long as you are in line by the time the polls close, the polling place will stay open to make sure everyone has the opportunity to vote.

There are many different kinds of paper ballots that can be used in the United States. Voters might be asked to bubble in their choice (like you do on a test at school), connect a line pointing to their choice, or punch a hole next to their choice.

NEW TECHNOLOGY allows some polling places to use computers during an election, so voters can use a touch screen feature to make their choice. This seems to be the preferred method, but many citizens believe that the chance of fraud or hacking with electronic voting is higher than with paper ballots.

WHAT KINDS OF ELECTIONS ARE THERE?

The presidential election is often seen as the most important because it is the highest elected office in the United States and it receives so much media coverage. But there are many other elections that have just as big of an impact on our lives as American citizens. It's important to stay informed about all of these elections and to cast your vote if you are eligible.

PRESIDENTIAL ELECTIONS occur every four years. The races on the ballot include the president and vice president, one-third of Senate seats, every House seat, and a variety of state elections and ballot measures, depending on the state. (These could include the governor, state senators and representatives, and even state supreme court judges.)

This election has the highest voter turnout (between 50 to 60 percent) because of the incredible amount of attention that is focused on the presidential race.

MIDTERM ELECTIONS occur two years before and two years after a presidential election, in even-numbered years. Similar to the presidential election, one-third of Senate seats and every House seat is up for election, along with the same variety of state elections and ballot measures. Voter turnout tends to be a little lower in midterm elections (usually between 40 and 50 percent) because the media coverage is not as intense as it is during a presidential year.

FACT

The midterm election in 2018 had the highest voter turnout since 1914, with 49.3% of registered voters casting their vote, including many young voters participating in an election for the first time.

Every state has its own method for how and when to fill a vacancy if a senator cannot complete his or her six-year term for any reason. Often, this is done with a **SPECIAL ELECTION**. The winner of a special election then serves out the remainder of the previous senator's term.

THE RESULTS OF ALL NATIONAL ELECTIONS DETERMINE:

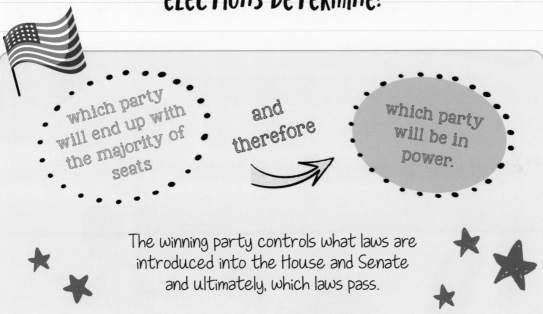

which party will end up with the majority of seats

and therefore

which party will be in power.

The winning party controls what laws are introduced into the House and Senate and ultimately, which laws pass.

A president can have a major impact on House and Senate elections. When the presidential election is on the ballot, voters tend to vote for House and Senate candidates from the same party as their preferred presidential candidate. This phenomenon is known as riding on presidential coattails. The reason this happens is because voters want the president to have a unified government, which will allow him or her to implement some of their policies.

The **COATTAIL EFFECT** usually works the opposite way during midterm elections, because the president tends to get blamed for anything that has gone wrong in the country during the first two years of his or her term. Voters can't vote the president out yet, so they vote against members of the president's party in the House and Senate races instead.

Every elected official at every level of government has a direct impact on the laws that govern us. That's why it is crucial to stay informed and put your support toward candidates who represent your views. Even if you are not eligible to vote yet, there are other ways you can stay involved in politics.

ELECTORAL COLLEGE

Voting is pretty straightforward for most roles in the government: Whoever gets the most votes wins. But this process is a little more complicated when voting for president. That's because **the winner of the presidential election is technically chosen by the Electoral College.**

The Electoral College is not a place where you enroll after high school. It is a system put in place by the founding fathers to determine who would be the president of the United States.

The Electoral College was established in the Constitution. It was a compromise between the president being elected by a vote in Congress or being elected by a popular vote of qualified citizens.

The founders were afraid to allow the people of the United States to choose a president directly. They didn't trust that the white male landowners who were eligible to vote at the time had enough knowledge to pick a capable leader. So they created the Electoral College in Article II of the Constitution as a backup plan. **The Electoral College was a compromise between the president being elected by Congress and being voted into office by qualified citizens.** This system meant that the president would be elected based on the <u>advice</u> of the people's vote, but the Electoral College voters, or **electors,** weren't required to pick the same person the people did.

Article II and the Twelfth Amendment mention "electors," but the term "Electoral College" doesn't actually appear in the Constitution!

HERE'S HOW IT WORKS

Each of the thirteen original colonies had its own election in which its citizens voted for who they wanted to be president. The electors from each state would then cast all of that state's electoral votes for the candidate who received the plurality, or the most votes, from the people of that state. The more populous the state, the more electoral votes it had. If a candidate received a majority of the total electoral votes, they were elected president of the United States.

The Electoral College works pretty much the same way today, but now there are more electors. As our population increased, so did the need to add more members of Congress. This in turn increased the size of the Electoral College.

The number of electors in the Electoral College has stayed the same since the passage of the Twenty-third Amendment in 1961. This gave Washington, DC, three electoral votes and brought the Electoral College up to 538 votes total.

In order to win the presidency, a candidate must receive 270 electoral votes.

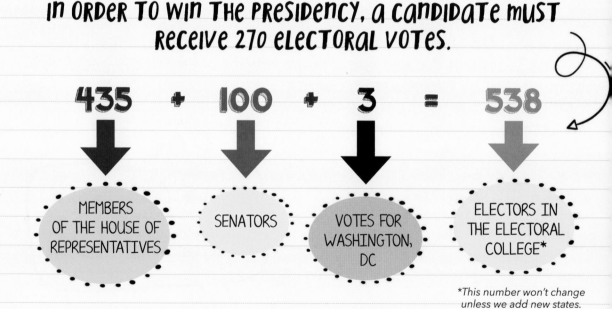

435 + **100** + **3** = **538**

| MEMBERS OF THE HOUSE OF REPRESENTATIVES | SENATORS | VOTES FOR WASHINGTON, DC | ELECTORS IN THE ELECTORAL COLLEGE* |

*This number won't change unless we add new states.

Even though the total number of electoral votes hasn't changed since 1961, the number of electoral votes for each state can change every ten years when the census is taken. Electoral votes are then revised to reflect the population changes in the United States.

The total number of electoral votes a state receives is equal to the number of members it has in the House of Representatives (which is based on population) plus two (representing its senators). For instance, Georgia has fourteen members of the House and two senators, so Georgia has sixteen electoral votes. California is the most populous state, and it has fifty-five electoral votes. The smallest states—with only three electoral votes each—are Alaska, Delaware, Montana, North Dakota, South Dakota, Vermont, and Wyoming. Remember, it's all about population, not geographic size. Alaska is the largest state in terms of land area, but it has the lowest number of electoral votes because of its small population.

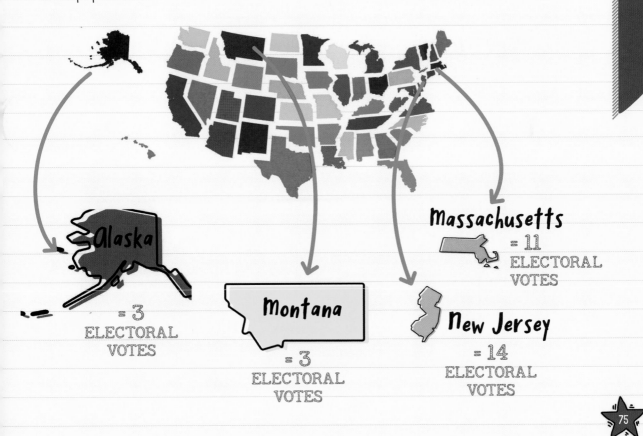

Alaska = 3 ELECTORAL VOTES

Montana = 3 ELECTORAL VOTES

Massachusetts = 11 ELECTORAL VOTES

New Jersey = 14 ELECTORAL VOTES

WINNING THE ELECTORAL COLLEGE

Every four years, when you vote for your candidate for president, you are actually voting for your candidate's electors.

Electors can be anyone except for current elected officials, and they are usually selected because of their loyalty to their political party (either Democrat or Republican).

For example, let's look at Florida, which has twenty-nine electoral votes. Before each presidential election, the Republicans and the Democrats both select twenty-nine Floridians to be their electors. **The candidate who wins the most votes in each state gets all of that state's electoral votes.** So if the Republican candidate wins the popular vote in the state of Florida, the twenty-nine electors selected by the Republicans become members of the Electoral College. These twenty-nine people then cast the official electoral votes for president. The electors submitted by the Democrats do not become members of the Electoral College and do not get to vote.

29

Florida

The Electoral College works a little differently in Nebraska and Maine, though. In these two states, instead of awarding all the electoral votes to the winner of the state, they award one vote to the winner of each district and two votes for whoever wins the overall popular vote of the state.

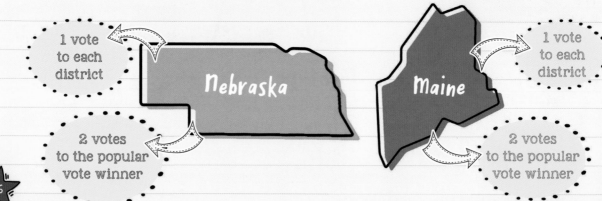

1 vote to each district

Nebraska

2 votes to the popular vote winner

1 vote to each district

Maine

2 votes to the popular vote winner

RED STATES AND BLUE STATES

Many states consistently support the same political party for president each year. The states that usually support the Democratic candidate are called **BLUE STATES**, and the states that usually support the Republican candidate are called **RED STATES**.

Generally, most of the South and the Midwest are considered red states, while most of the northeastern and West Coast states are blue states.

As of 2016, Ohio has correctly predicted the winner of the last thirteen presidential elections— voting for the Republican candidate seven times and the Democratic candidate six times.

FACT

These can change from year to year.

SWING STATES

In recent years, most presidential elections have been decided by a few key states known as swing states. These states get their nickname because they "swing" between parties from one election to the next, and they are not considered reliable states for the Democrats or the Republicans to win. Both presidential candidates and their parties spend the most time and money campaigning in the swing states to try to bring them over to their side. That's why these states are also sometimes called **BATTLEGROUND STATES.**

Some common battleground states: Arizona, Colorado, Florida, Iowa, Michigan, Nevada, New Hampshire, North Carolina, Ohio, Pennsylvania, Virginia, and Wisconsin.

LET'S GO WIN THE PRESIDENCY

When the presidential candidates are planning their election strategies, they take out a map and figure out a path to win 270 electoral votes. Because of the "winner takes all" feature of the Electoral College, both parties have a pretty good idea of which states they will most likely win based on how that state has voted in the past. For example, the state of New York has voted for the Democratic candidate in every election since 1984, and Alabama has voted Republican in every election since 1980.

Then the candidates start campaigning! Both candidates will crisscross the nation, spending more time in swing states they know they need to win in order to reach the magic number of 270 electoral votes. They usually spend little time and money campaigning in states that they know will vote for their opponent. Remember, it doesn't matter if you lose in a state by two votes or two million— the winner receives all of the electoral votes for that state.

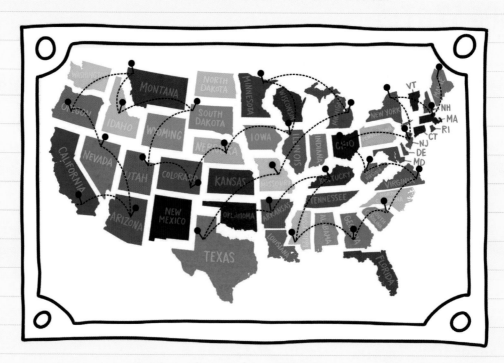

WHaT IF no one wins a majority?

If no candidate receives at least 270 electoral votes, then the winner of the presidential election is decided by the House of Representatives. This duty falls to the House because its members have always been directly elected by the people.

Every state gets to cast one vote. The representatives from each state meet in a group and decide who their state will vote for. Their choice is usually determined along party lines. So if a state has more Democratic members, they will vote for the Democratic candidate, and if they have more Republicans, they will choose the Republican candidate.

Whichever candidate receives at least twenty-six votes from the House of Representatives becomes the next president of the United States.

The vice president is determined separately in the Senate. This is because in the Constitution, one of the VP's responsibilities is to serve as president of the Senate. Each senator casts one vote, and the winner becomes the vice president, alongside the president chosen by the House.

FACT

Since the president and vice president are chosen separately if there is no winner in the Electoral College, the two winners could be from different political parties! But this hasn't happened since the passage of the Twelfth Amendment.

79

Time for Change?

Because the winner of the presidential election is really selected by the Electoral College, many people are angry when the winner of the national **popular vote** doesn't become the president. In the 2016 election, the Democratic candidate, Hillary Clinton, won the popular vote by almost three million votes. But since Donald Trump won more than 270 electoral votes, he became the president instead. This large gap in the votes caused a renewed desire to change the electoral process for choosing the president.

Since the Electoral College was created in the original US Constitution, it would take a Constitutional amendment to change this system.

More than 700 proposals have been introduced in Congress over the past 200 years with suggestions for updating or eliminating the Electoral College system. There have been more proposals for constitutional amendments about the Electoral College than on any other subject! However, none of these have been sent to the states for a vote of acceptance.

PROS and CONS of the electoral college

Here are some of the arguments for and against the Electoral College.

FOR:

⭐ Reduces the costs of national campaigns

⭐ Keeps high-population states from deciding the presidency. Without it, a big vote margin in one state (like California or Texas) could determine the winner of the entire election.

AGAINST:

⭐ The winner of the election may not receive the most popular votes. As of 2016, this has happened five times.

⭐ Some electoral votes count more than others. In 2012, Wyoming had less than 200,000 people per each of its three electoral votes but Texas had almost 700,000 people per each of its 38 electoral votes.

⭐ Causes the elections to focus on swing states such as Florida and Ohio.

WHAT DOES THE PRESIDENT DO?

It's a long, hard process to become president of the United States—and not just anyone can do it! It's the highest elected job in the United States, so anyone who wants to serve as president has to meet some requirements first. In order to run for this office, a candidate must be at least **THIRTY-FIVE YEARS OLD**, a **NATURAL-BORN CITIZEN** of the United States, and a **FOURTEEN-YEAR RESIDENT** of the United States.

Even if they meet all of those requirements, the president has a **BIG** job. Whoever fills this role has to be prepared to take on all of its duties and more.

PRESIDENTIAL SEAL

POWERS OF THE PRESIDENT

The president is the head of the executive branch. He or she has many "formal powers," which are given to them by the Constitution.

SOME OF THE PRESIDENT'S FORMAL POWERS INCLUDE:

DOMESTIC

★ signing or vetoing laws

★ pardoning felons

★ nominating federal judges

★ appointing heads of executive agencies

FOREIGN POLICY

★ being commander in chief of the US Armed Forces

★ negotiating treaties

★ acting as head of state by greeting foreign leaders

The president also has powers that are not granted in the Constitution. One of these powers is being the leader of their political party. The president is the most well-known elected official in the United States, so it makes sense that they would be the leader of the party they represent. The president uses their platform, sometimes called a bully pulpit, to spread their message to the country—and to the world. The bully pulpit is the president's use of all forms of the media to try to persuade the public to support his or her ideas. From FDR's fireside chats to President Trump's Twitter account, the president has always used the media as a means to communicate with the world.

Other presidential powers include the ability to keep national security secrets from the public, known as executive privilege, and the ability to change the way an executive agency applies a law, called an executive order.

FACT

President Truman desegregated the US military through an executive order in 1948.

83

PRESIDENTS OF THE

Number	Name	Political Party	Years in Office
1	GEORGE WASHINGTON	n/a	1789–1797
2	JOHN ADAMS	Federalist	1797–1801
3	THOMAS JEFFERSON	Democratic-Republican	1801–1809
4	JAMES MADISON	Democratic-Republican	1809–1817
5	JAMES MONROE	Democratic-Republican	1817–1825
6	JOHN QUINCY ADAMS	Democratic-Republican	1825–1829
7	ANDREW JACKSON	Democrat	1829–1837
8	MARTIN VAN BUREN	Democrat	1837–1841
9	WILLIAM HENRY HARRISON	Whig	March–April 1841
10	JOHN TYLER	Whig	1841–1845

UNITED STATES

Number	Name	Political Party	Years in Office
11	JAMES K. POLK	Democrat	1845–1849
12	ZACHARY TAYLOR	Whig	1849–1850
13	MILLARD FILLMORE	Whig	1850–1853
14	FRANKLIN PIERCE	Democrat	1853–1857
15	JAMES BUCHANAN	Democrat	1857–1861
16	ABRAHAM LINCOLN	Republican	1861–1865
17	ANDREW JOHNSON	Democrat	1865–1869
18	ULYSSES S. GRANT	Republican	1869–1877
19	RUTHERFORD B. HAYES	Republican	1877–1881
20	JAMES A. GARFIELD	Republican	March–September 1881

Number	Name	Political Party	Years in Office
21	CHESTER A. ARTHUR	Republican	1881–1885
22	GROVER CLEVELAND	Democrat	1885–1889
23	BENJAMIN HARRISON	Republican	1889–1893
24	GROVER CLEVELAND	Democrat	1893–1897
25	WILLIAM MCKINLEY	Republican	1897–1901
26	THEODORE ROOSEVELT	Republican	1901–1909
27	WILLIAM H. TAFT	Republican	1909–1913
28	WOODROW WILSON	Democrat	1913–1921
29	WARREN G. HARDING	Republican	1921–1923
30	CALVIN COOLIDGE	Republican	1923–1929
31	HERBERT HOOVER	Republican	1929–1933
32	FRANKLIN D. ROOSEVELT	Democrat	1933–1945
33	HARRY S TRUMAN	Democrat	1945–1953

Number	Name	Political Party	Years in Office
34	DWIGHT D. EISENHOWER	Republican	1953–1961
35	JOHN F. KENNEDY	Democrat	1961–1963
36	LYNDON B. JOHNSON	Democrat	1963–1969
37	RICHARD NIXON	Republican	1969–1974
38	GERALD FORD	Republican	1974–1977
39	JIMMY CARTER	Democrat	1977–1981
40	RONALD REAGAN	Republican	1981–1989
41	GEORGE H. W. BUSH	Republican	1989–1993
42	BILL CLINTON	Democrat	1993–2001
43	GEORGE W. BUSH	Republican	2001–2009
44	BARACK OBAMA	Democrat	2009–2017
45	DONALD TRUMP	Republican	2017–
46	????	????	????

THE PRESIDENT'S TEAM

The president's White House staff are his closest advisors. The staff is usually made up of people who helped the president get elected. His or her closest ally is the **CHIEF OF STAFF**. This person controls access to the president and tries to handle any issues within the White House before they reach the president. The chief of staff is also a sounding board for the president to bounce ideas off before a final decision is made.

The president also employs **SPEECHWRITERS** and **DOMESTIC AND FOREIGN POLICY ADVISORS** to help make critical decisions and present them to the public. The **PRESS SECRETARY** is responsible for letting the media know what the administration has done (and why) and for answering questions on the president's behalf about events that have occurred. These press briefings allow the White House to control the way a story is presented to the public.

WHAT IF SOMETHING HAPPENS TO THE PRESIDENT?

The president has so many responsibilities that our country wouldn't be able to run without someone doing this job. That's why the country passed the Twenty-fifth Amendment in 1967.

This amendment lists the **order of succession** if the president dies, resigns, or is removed from office during his or her term. It explains who would take over the job until the next presidential election.

HERE'S THE COMPLETE LIST!

1. Vice president
2. Speaker of the House
3. President pro tempore of the Senate
4. Secretary of State
5. Secretary of the Treasury
6. Secretary of Defense
7. Attorney General
8. Secretary of the Interior
9. Secretary of Agriculture
10. Secretary of Commerce
11. Secretary of Labor
12. Secretary of Health and Human Services
13. Secretary of Housing and Urban Development
14. Secretary of Transportation
15. Secretary of Energy
16. Secretary of Education
17. Secretary of Veterans Affairs
18. Secretary of Homeland Security

The list goes all the way through the cabinet (in the order in which the departments were created) just in case. But we've never had to go past VP on the list before!

When a new president steps in to take over the job, they have to nominate a new person to fill the role of vice president. Their nomination then has to be confirmed by the Senate.

WHICH PRESIDENTS DIDN'T FINISH THEIR TERMS?

WILLIAM HENRY HARRISON
Died in April 1841, only 31 days into office

ZACHARY TAYLOR
Died in July 1850, after less than a year and half in office

ABRAHAM LINCOLN
Assassinated in April 1865, one month into his second term

JAMES GARFIELD
Died in September 1881, due to complications from an earlier assassination attempt, after only seven months in office

WARREN G. HARDING
Died in August 1923, after about two-and-a-half years in office

FRANKLIN D. ROOSEVELT
Died in April 1945, less than three months into his fourth term

JOHN F. KENNEDY
Assassinated in November 1963, after nearly three years in office

RICHARD NIXON
Resigned in August 1974, less than two years into his second term

TAKING OFFICE

Presidential elections are held in November, but the new president does not officially take office until **JANUARY 20TH** of the following year.

In the time between the election and the inauguration, the `president elect` and his or her transition team work closely with the outgoing president's team to make sure the transfer of power goes smoothly.

> The time period between the election and the new president taking over is known as the **lame-duck period** for the US government. Very little work gets done during these few months, because many of the elected officials (sometimes including the president) have lost their reelection bids and are preparing to leave office. The lame-duck period used to be longer—lasting from November until March! It was officially shortened in 1937 with the passage of the Twentieth Amendment.

On **INAUGURATION DAY**, usually millions of people gather to watch the president elect take the oath of office and officially be sworn in as president of the United States. The new president delivers a speech in front of the US Capitol building about their goals for the coming term. Then he or she rides from the Capitol to the White House, while citizens line the streets to get a glimpse of the new first family.

THE 2009 PRESIDENTIAL INAUGURATION

91

STATE OF THE UNION

One of the president's other duties is delivering the annual State of the Union address. This message is given by the president each year to a **joint session** of Congress. A joint session of Congress is one of the rare occasions when all 100 senators and 435 House members gather together. This occurs at the beginning of each calendar year in office.

This speech allows the president to inform the American public what his or her plans are for the upcoming year. It highlights the president's **LEGISLATIVE ACHIEVEMENTS** and includes an **ECONOMIC REPORT** for the nation. The speech usually lasts around an hour, but it is frequently interrupted by members of Congress who give the president multiple standing ovations for his or her policy ideas and accomplishments.

PRESIDENT BARACK OBAMA GETS A STANDING OVATION DELIVERING THE STATE OF THE UNION ADDRESS ON JANUARY 27, 2010.

The opposing party usually chooses one of their own party leaders to respond to the State of the Union. They might choose a governor from a big state or a member of Congress who is well known. They will give a brief rebuttal and explain their party's ideas of what the government should be focusing on. (This usually contradicts what the president says in his or her address.)

The Constitution specifically requires the president to give Congress this kind of update periodically. During the early years of the Republic, the president usually just submitted a written report to Congress. That changed in 1913 when Woodrow Wilson, the twenty-eighth president, delivered his address to Congress in person to try to rally support for his agenda. The practice stuck. Now, with radio, television, and the Internet, the State of the Union address is broadcast live across the country and the world.

PRESIDENT WOODROW WILSON SPEAKING TO CONGRESS, DECEMBER 2, 1918

IMPEACHMENT

The president has a lot of power and responsibility, but that does not mean they are above the law. He or she can be held accountable if they take advantage of their position or abuse their power. If this occurs, a formal charge of impeachment can be brought against the president.

Impeachment is a formal accusation of wrongdoing against a public official. The president, vice president, and all other civil officers of the United States can be removed from office if they are impeached and convicted of crimes like treason, bribery, and obstruction of justice.

The House of Representatives can impeach, or bring charges against, the president with a simple majority vote. Then an investigation usually takes place in the **HOUSE JUDICIARY COMMITTEE**. This committee calls witnesses and hears testimony about the possible wrongdoings of the president.

If the majority of House members agree that the president did things that are outside of his or her power, they can officially bring **ARTICLES OF IMPEACHMENT** against the president.

Once an impeachment charge is filed, the Senate holds a trial where they consider evidence and hear witness testimony, with the chief justice of the United States as the presiding judge. The Senate then votes on whether the president is guilty of the charges presented. **To remove the president from office, two-thirds of all senators must vote to remove.**

Presidents Andrew Johnson, Bill Clinton, and Donald Trump were all impeached by the House of Representatives. But none of these presidents were removed after their trials in the Senate.

THE VICE PRESIDENT

But what about the vice president? What exactly is their job? The vice president is the only elected official who has a role in both the executive and legislative branches. He or she is the **SECOND-HIGHEST-RANKING** officer in the executive branch, and they are first in line to take over if something happens to the president.

The vice president is also the **PRESIDENT OF THE SENATE**. If a tie occurs during a Senate vote, the VP is the tiebreaker. Vice presidents have been given a lot more responsibilities by the president over the last few decades. He or she now helps the president with their policy proposals and advises the president on foreign and domestic issues, too.

John Adams

THE FIRST LADY (AND FIRST GENTLEMAN)

First Lady of the United States is the title held by the host of the White House, historically the **WIFE OF THE PRESIDENT** of the United States. She organizes and attends official ceremonies and functions of state either along with, or in place of, the president. In recent years, the first lady has supported causes such as volunteerism, women's rights, childhood literacy, and reducing childhood obesity.

Abigail Adams

Eleanor Roosevelt

Jacqueline Kennedy

Laura Bush

Michelle Obama

This responsibility of White House host could also fall to a **First Gentleman**, if future presidents have a husband instead of a wife.

FACT

James Buchanan was the only president who never married. His niece Harriet Lane served as his official First Lady while he was in office.

97

WHAT HAPPENS IN CONGRESS?

When most people think about the United States government, they automatically think of the president. The president does hold the highest office in the country, and they represent our country on the world stage. But that doesn't mean that the president is the most powerful part of our government. That title belongs to Congress.

WHAT DOES CONGRESS LOOK LIKE?

When the founding fathers created the three branches of government, they intended for the legislative branch to have the most power. That's why so much of the Constitution is taken up by Article I, which sets up this part of the government. Article I is the same length as the other six articles in the Constitution combined!

The United States Congress is made up of two chambers. Since the United States gained its independence from Great Britain, our leaders got many of their ideas about government from how things worked in England. The British Parliament had two chambers, so the founding fathers created a bicameral legislature, too. In the United States, this was comprised of the House of Representatives and the Senate.

Once they figured out the structure of the legislative branch, the biggest issue facing the founding fathers was determining how to allocate the seats in each chamber. The Constitutional Convention was comprised of delegates from twelve of the original thirteen states. (Rhode Island boycotted the convention and did not attend.) But the delegates were divided. Those from small states requested that representation in Congress be the same for every state, no matter how many people lived in it. But those from big states believed that they deserved more representation since they had more voters; they requested the seats be allocated based on population.

Rhode Island

This disagreement provided the perfect opportunity for compromise. In the end, the framers of the Constitution determined that the small states would get their equal representation in the Senate, and the big states would get their representation based on population in the House of Representatives.

Read more about how many people are in Congress on page 103.

A bicameral legislature also has another advantage. This organization creates its own system of checks and balances. Neither the House nor Senate can pass a bill without the other's consent. This means passing a law requires a lot of cooperation within Congress, and it encourages compromise between the two chambers.

POWERS OF CONGRESS

Congress was given the most powers in the Constitution—but what exactly are they?

Congress's most important power is its ability to **MAKE LAWS**. A bill only becomes a law after it passes in both the House and the Senate and then is signed by the president. If the president denies the law with a veto, Congress can vote to override the veto and pass the law without the president's signature. Both the House and the Senate need to have at least two-thirds of their members vote to override the veto to make this happen, so presidential vetoes are overridden less than 5 percent of the time.

Read more about exactly how a law is passed on page 110.

Congress has the power to **LAY AND COLLECT TAXES** to provide for the common defense and for the country's general welfare. This means that the money collected from taxes will be spent by the government for the health, peace, and safety of its citizens.

Congress was also given the power to **COIN AND BORROW MONEY**. The power to coin money means that only the federal government can produce the currency that is used in the country. The power to borrow money is essential for the survival of any government. Governments are designed to provide benefits for their citizens; usually in peacetime, these expenses cost less than the government collects in taxes. However, if a country's expenses go up— during a war, for instance—the government needs to be able to borrow money from another country. Like most countries, the combination of wars and economic crises have led the United States to borrow more than it takes in, causing the country to go into debt.

The commerce clause allows Congress to **REGULATE TRADE**, both between states and with foreign nations. This clause also allows Congress to have authority over any economic activity in the United States that occurs across state lines. Congress has used this clause over the years to regulate a variety of industries and investigate injustices that might be occurring in a state. For instance, many businesses in southern states were either fined or threatened with being shut down if they were found to be discriminating against African Americans after the passage of the Civil Rights Act of 1964.

The Constitution gives Congress the power to **CREATE ALL FEDERAL COURTS BELOW THE SUPREME COURT**. The federal court system allows anyone accused of a federal crime to have a fair trial, similar to how the state court system works. Federal courts also give the accused the ability to **appeal** a losing verdict from a regional appeals court.

Read more about the federal court system on page 121.

Congress was also given the power to **RAISE AN ARMY** and the **POWER TO DECLARE WAR**. This was a clear break from how the monarchies in Europe worked at the time, since kings and queens had the authority to declare war on their own. But the founding fathers granted this power to Congress instead of the president. They did not want the United States to enter into a conflict without careful deliberation and debate from its elected officials, rather than just one person's decision.

Congress decides the **REQUIREMENTS FOR BECOMING A CITIZEN** of the United States, including determining who has the right to participate in the government. Over the years, Congress has extended the right to vote to African Americans, women, and any citizen over the age of eighteen. Congress also decides the steps that need to be taken for an immigrant to become an American citizen.

The Constitution gives Congress the authority to **IMPEACH AND REMOVE ANY ELECTED OR APPOINTED OFFICIALS** in the United States who have engaged in treason, bribery, or other crimes. The House brings the impeachment charges against the accused official, and the Senate holds the trial to remove the elected official. Federal judges can also face articles of impeachment.

Read more about impeachment on page 94.

The last of Congress's major powers comes from the necessary and proper clause in the Constitution, also known as the elastic clause. This clause gives Congress the power to **DO WHATEVER IT DEEMS NECESSARY TO HELP CARRY OUT POWERS THAT IT WAS GIVEN IN ARTICLE I** of the Constitution.

For example, Congress used this clause to create the United States National Bank. This was allowed, even though it was not a specific power given to Congress, because the bank aided Congress in carrying out other powers given to them, like coining money, regulating trade, and collecting taxes.

THE HOUSE OF REPRESENTATIVES VS. THE SENATE

CONGRESS is granted certain powers by the Constitution, but each chamber is granted its own individual powers as well.

HOUSE OF REPRESENTATIVES:

★ Made up of 435 members dispersed among the fifty states.

★ Members serve two-year terms.

★ Members each represent a district of approximately 700,000 people.

★ Anyone who runs for a House seat must be at least twenty-five years old, must have been a citizen of the United States for at least seven years, and must live in the state that they will represent.

★ The unique powers of the House include the ability to bring impeachment charges, introduce any law that entails spending taxpayer money, and select the president if no candidate wins the majority of votes in the Electoral College.

SEE NEXT PAGE FOR MORE!

Senate:

★ Made up of two senators from each state (one hundred senators total).

★ Senators serve six-year terms, and they represent their entire state.

★ To run for senator, a candidate must be at least thirty years old, must have been a citizen of the United States for at least nine years, and must live in the state that they will represent.

★ The unique powers of the Senate include holding impeachment trials, ratifying treaties, confirming presidential appointments, and choosing the vice president if there is no winner in the Electoral College.

Congress has two one-year sessions during each two-year term. Their schedule is similar to a school calendar. They are off on holidays (like Martin Luther King, Jr. Day), have two weeks off for a "spring break" in April, most of August off for summer vacation, and they break for the winter holidays during the last couple weeks of December. They use a lot of their time off in their individual districts or states to meet with their constituents and also to campaign in an election year.

CONGRESSIONAL SESSIONS BEGIN ON JANUARY 3 each year, when the representatives and senators meet separately at the US Capitol building. The Constitution mandates that Congress convene at noon on January 3, unless the preceding Congress designated a different day.

JANUARY
3

Congress follows a regular routine on the opening day of each new session, including **SWEARING IN NEWLY ELECTED OR REELECTED MEMBERS** from the latest election. The new congresspeople come to a unanimous agreement about when bills may begin to be introduced. If there is a vacancy or a change in party control, they also **ELECT THE NEW PARTY LEADERS**.

Other first-day activities may occur, such as **WELCOMING REMARKS** from the minority party and majority party leaders, and calling a meeting with all of the House and Senate present to officially count the electoral votes after a presidential election. Committee assignments are also given out to the newly elected Congress.

MEMBERS OF THE US HOUSE OF REPRESENTATIVES ARE SWORN IN ON CAPITOL HILL ON JANUARY 3, 2019.

WHAT ARE CONGRESSIONAL COMMITTEES?

One of the biggest day-to-day responsibilities for people serving in Congress is being a part of a congressional committee. Each member of the House and the Senate usually serves on a few different committees. These committees are divided by policy areas. They are used to **IDENTIFY ISSUES** that could change current policies or create new ones, and then they **RECOMMEND A COURSE OF ACTION** for the issue to the rest of the chamber.

TYPES OF COMMITTEES

There are three different kinds of congressional committees: standing committees, select committees, and joint committees.

STANDING COMMITTEES are the only permanent congressional committees. This is **where all of the work gets done on a bill.** The bill gets changed and amended until it is ready for the full chamber to vote on it. Most bills (over 90 percent) never make it out of the standing committee because the members do not believe that there will be enough support for the bill from the entire chamber.

SELECT COMMITTEES (or special committees) are temporary committees; they are created to deal with issues that are not covered directly by any standing committee. Select committees are generally formed to carry out investigations rather than to write legislation. For instance, in 1972, the Senate created the Senate Select Committee on Presidential Campaign Activities to investigate the Watergate scandal.

JOINT COMMITTEES are made up of members of both the House and the Senate. They are formed to bring attention to a larger issue, and they are often for investigative purposes. One type of joint committee, called a joint conference committee, may be formed after a proposed bill has passed in both chambers. The members of the conference committee work together to figure out how to balance the differences between the House's version of the bill and the Senate's. It's the joint conference committee's job to produce a final bill (a compromise between the two standing committees' bills) that can be voted on in both chambers.

KEY STANDING COMMITTEES

There are around fifteen to twenty standing committees in both the House and the Senate.

APPROPRIATIONS COMMITTEES in both the House and Senate are responsible for allocating the necessary funds to any bill passed.

THE JUDICIARY COMMITTEE in the Senate evaluates federal judges for confirmation. Its counterpart in the House brings impeachment charges against officials if necessary.

THE ARMED SERVICES COMMITTEE is a Senate committee responsible for investigating any action taken by the United States military.

THE WAYS AND MEANS COMMITTEE in the House is responsible for writing tax laws.

THE RULES COMMITTEE is a powerful committee in the House that allows the Speaker to control which legislation makes it to the floor for a vote.

HOW DO YOU GET ON A COMMITTEE?

Committees can be wildly different in size. Some of the more popular committees, like House Foreign Affairs, has nearly fifty members, while the House Ethics Committee usually has just ten members. The majority party at the time (either Republicans or Democrats) always has more members in congressional committees. That way, they control all of the votes throughout the lawmaking process. This, in turn, dictates which bills progress through the committees and, ultimately, how the bills are written.

Members of Congress try to get on a committee that deals with legislation that directly affects their voters. For instance, a senator or house representative from Kansas might try to get on the Agriculture Committee because many residents of Kansas are farmers. The elected official would then be able to help write legislation that will directly impact the lives or his or her voters.

Committees that are in the news a lot are also desired by members of Congress because it can make a congressperson more well-known. For example, when a conflict arises with another country, the members of the Senate Intelligence Committee will be interviewed by various media for their expert opinion, and in turn, their name recognition will increase with prospective voters.

Representatives who have been in Congress the longest have the first choice of committee assignments every two years, at the start of a new term. It usually takes a few terms in either chamber to get on all the committees that you want.

The leader of a congressional committee is called the **chair**. You can only be the chair of one committee at a time. The chair is always someone from the majority party (or the party that rules Congress at the moment)—usually the most **senior** person from that party who is on that committee.

All leadership positions in the House and Senate are typically based on seniority, although anyone can compete for any position within each chamber.

HOW A BILL BECOMES A LAW

The work these committees do is important, because they are drafting the bills that might end up becoming our future laws. But drafting the bill is only the first step in a long, complicated lawmaking process.

STEP 1:

The idea for a bill can come from anybody, but only a senator or representative can introduce a bill in Congress. The Constitution gives the House of Representatives sole power to introduce revenue bills, but either chamber can introduce any other type of bill. Bills can affect the majority of Americans or just a small segment of the country, depending on the issue they are trying to address.

STEP 2:

Once a bill is introduced, it gets sent to the standing committee that it most relates to. For instance, any bill having to do with farming would be sent to the Agriculture Committee. The standing committees hold hearings on the bill and hear from experts on the issues relating to the proposed legislation. The bill goes through a series of changes as members of the committee attempt to create a bill that has a chance to be passed by the entire chamber.

Learn more about standing committees on page 108.

STEP 2 CONTINUED

But those aren't the only changes that happen to the bill during this stage. Since the political party that is in power controls the votes within the committee, they also have the ability to craft the bill however they see fit. They can vote for changes that get the bill closer to their vision of what the law should be. During this process, 90 percent of bills die, because members realize that there is not enough support within the committee or from the whole chamber to pass the proposed legislation. However, if the bill is completed and the committee (and its majority party members) vote that it is ready for passage, the bill is finally sent to the full chamber for review.

At this point, the two chambers have slightly different processes for reviewing and voting on bills.

STEP 3A:
In the House, most bills go to the Rules Committee, where two things happen:

1. A time limit for the length of debate in the full House is set, usually no more than an hour for both the proponents and opponents of a bill.

2. The bill is either marked open (which means that changes can be proposed by non-committee members) or closed (changes are forbidden by anyone outside of the committee).

THERE'S MORE!

STEP 3B:

In the Senate, the rules are much more relaxed. There is no time limit for the debate of a new bill, and additions (called **riders**) can be added by any senator. A rider is an addition to a bill that does not directly relate to the subject matter of the bill. For example, a bill being voted on to fund hospitals can have a rider attached to it that gives money to clean up the subway system in New York City.

Since there are no time limits for the debate of a bill, the minority party in the Senate might try to **filibuster** a bill they do not want to pass. A filibuster is a delay tactic of continued talking to try to prevent a bill from ever being voted on.

During a filibuster, a senator will spend hours talking to the chamber about why the bill should fail. They usually start by explaining the problems with the proposed legislation and the negative impact of passing it. As the filibuster continues, the senator might do silly things like read poetry, sing songs, or recite Dr. Seuss books. He or she is not required to directly discuss the actual legislation, as long as they don't stop talking during the filibuster.

In order to prevent a filibuster, the majority party can call for a vote of **cloture** before the discussion begins. A successful cloture requires three-fifths of senators (normally sixty) to vote to disallow filibusters. If it passes, the Senate is referred to as filibuster proof. But a cloture doesn't happen often. It is very hard to get sixty votes in the Senate; it is rare for one of the two major parties to have control of that many seats, and it is even more rare for someone to vote to invoke cloture against a member of their own party.

STEP 4:

Once the committee and non-committee members have finished debating the bill, then the full House or Senate votes yes or no on the bill.

The chambers vote individually on the legislation. The bill must pass with a majority vote in both the House and the Senate in order for it to be sent to the president. If either chamber fails to pass the bill, the bill is dead, and the process is over.

STEP 5:

The president has three options when he or she receives a bill from Congress:

1. He or she signs it into law.

2. He or she uses the power of veto, rejecting the bill, and sends it back to Congress for a possible override. Congress can overturn a presidential veto if two-thirds of the House and two-thirds of the Senate all vote to pass the bill anyway. (But this happens less than 5 percent of the time.)

3. He or she holds on to the bill for ten days and hopes Congress will depart for the end of their session. If Congress adjourns, then a pocket veto has occurred and the bill dies. If Congress remains in session, the bill becomes a law without the president's signature after the ten days have passed.

CHECK THIS OUT!

HOW A BILL BECOMES A LAW
(chart edition!)

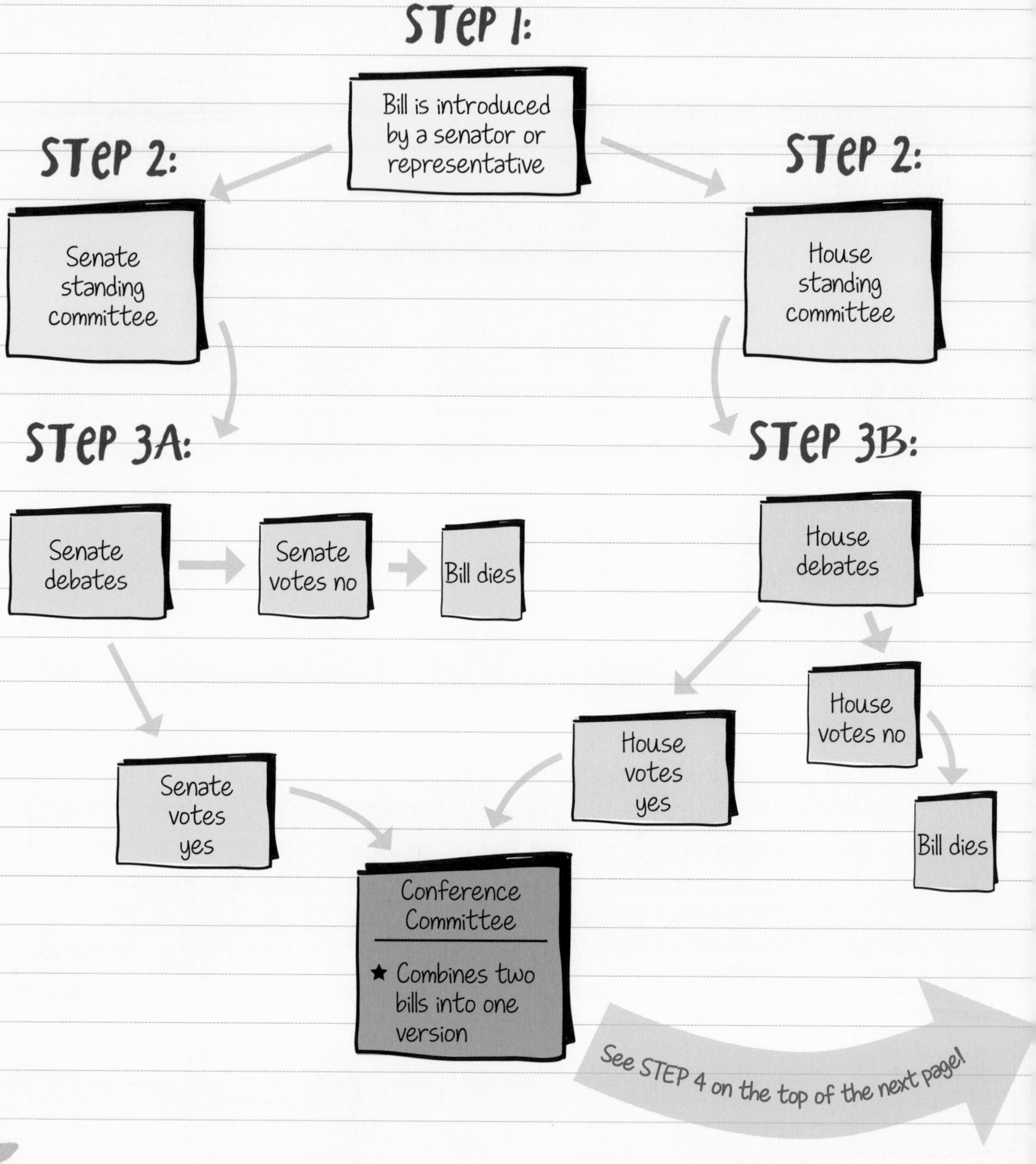

STEP 1:

Bill is introduced by a senator or representative

STEP 2:

Senate standing committee

STEP 2:

House standing committee

STEP 3A:

Senate debates → Senate votes no → Bill dies

Senate votes yes

STEP 3B:

House debates

House votes no

House votes yes

Bill dies

Conference Committee

★ Combines two bills into one version

See STEP 4 on the top of the next page!

STEP 4:

Full Senate votes

Senate votes no

Senate votes yes

Bill dies

STEP 4:

Full House votes

House votes yes

House votes no

Bill dies

STEP 5:

Bill is sent to the president

President signs the bill into law

President vetos the bill

President sits on the bill for ten days

Congress overturns the veto with a two-thirds vote in the House and the Senate

Bill dies

Congress adjourns & the bill is pocket vetoed

Congress remains in session

Bill becomes law

Bill dies

Bill becomes law without the president's signature

WHAT ARE INTEREST GROUPS?

There are many people who pay close attention to the lawmaking process. These different groups want to make sure that the government is passing or defeating bills that correspond with their ideals. Groups of people who share a common goal about how laws should be written are called interest groups. Their goal is to ensure that any public policy that becomes law will be written in a way that benefits their group. Interest groups can be formed based on a common bond such as race, religion, age, occupation, or gender, or just based on a mutual interest in an issue.

★ WELL-KNOWN INTEREST GROUPS ★

AMERICAN MEDICAL ASSOCIATION (1847)

Its mission is to promote the art and science of medicine and the betterment of public health.

NATIONAL RIFLE ASSOCIATION (1871)

The NRA is a gun rights advocacy group that protects the rights of people to keep and bear arms.

SIERRA CLUB (1892)

This group's goal is to educate and ask citizens to protect and restore the quality of the environment and to use any legal means to carry out this goal.

| NAACP (1909) | The NAACP (National Association for the Advancement of Colored People) was formed to ensure the political, educational, social, and economic equality of rights of all persons and to eliminate race-based discrimination. |

| THE HERITAGE FOUNDATION (1973) | Its mission is to promote free enterprise, limited government, individual freedom, traditional American values, and a strong national defense. |

| MARCH FOR OUR LIVES (2018) | This group harnesses the power of young people across the country to fight for sensible gun violence prevention policies that save lives. |

HOW DO INTEREST GROUPS AFFECT WHICH BILLS BECOME LAWS?

Interest groups use many techniques to try to influence public policy and impact which bills become laws.

One of the most popular methods used by interest groups is **lobbying**. This is the practice of providing specific information to lawmakers and other elected officials about the possible effects of the proposed legislation. A lobbyist might simply let a legislator know the harmful effects that the legislation might have on their community if the bill passes.

But sometimes lobbyists might prove their point in a different way. Their information might be presented as a threat or consequence for the elected official voting the "wrong" way. For instance, a lobbyist might warn a congressperson that if they don't stop a certain bill, the members of the interest group they represent might work to vote them out of office.

Campaign contributions are money that is given to candidates by individuals or groups who support their ideas. By donating to a candidate, the interest group may hope to get a future meeting with the candidate if he or she wins the election, as a thank you for supporting their campaign.

Another goal of supporting candidates with campaign contributions is to elect as many candidates as possible who share the same beliefs as the interest group. This would make it easier to gain access to and influence the elected officials, since they share similar views on government.

Litigation means using the court system to stop or defend policies based on a group's interests. For example, the NAACP used the court system to end segregation in schools. Mass mobilization is when large groups of people gather together to raise awareness for a cause, like the March For Our Lives events that took place in 2018. The intended goal of mass mobilization is to change policy to benefit their group.

While there are many different ways for individuals and interest groups to show which bills they support and oppose, in the end, it is still up to the members of Congress to make the final call. They can use the information they receive from their constituents, lobbyists, and other members of their party in order to figure out which way they should vote. This power is why it is so important for citizens to stay informed and to make sure that their elected officials are creating laws that will do the most good for our country.

WHAT IS THE SUPREME COURT?

From the beginning of our nation, it seemed that the judicial branch would be the least important of the three branches of American government. The Articles of Confederation failed to create courts or even mention the idea of a national judiciary. However, when writing the Constitution, the founders thought it was essential to create this third branch of government.

The judicial system in America had already been established as each of the thirteen colonies had its own court system based on the British common-law model. The founders decided to create a **DUAL COURT SYSTEM**, with courts both at the national and state level. Article III created the Supreme Court as the highest court in the land and gave Congress the power to establish any inferior courts.

The Judiciary Act of 1789 set up the federal court system and the guidelines for the operation of the Supreme Court, which originally had just six justices (or judges). The federal judiciary was established as a three-tiered system. The duties of these different tiers changed over the years, up until the passage of the Judiciary Act of 1869. Since then, the duties of the three levels of federal courts have remained the same.

The trial courts are called **DISTRICT COURTS**, appeals are heard in the **CIRCUIT COURTS**, and the **SUPREME COURT** remains the highest tier in the federal judiciary, reviewing cases that come up from the lower tiers.

Since the Supreme Court is the highest court in the federal judiciary, it serves as the court of last resort. Any decisions made by the Supreme Court are final and cannot be appealed. It is the court's job to protect the civil rights and civil liberties of United States citizens by striking down laws that violate the Constitution.

THIS IS HOW THE US COURT SYSTEM WORKS:

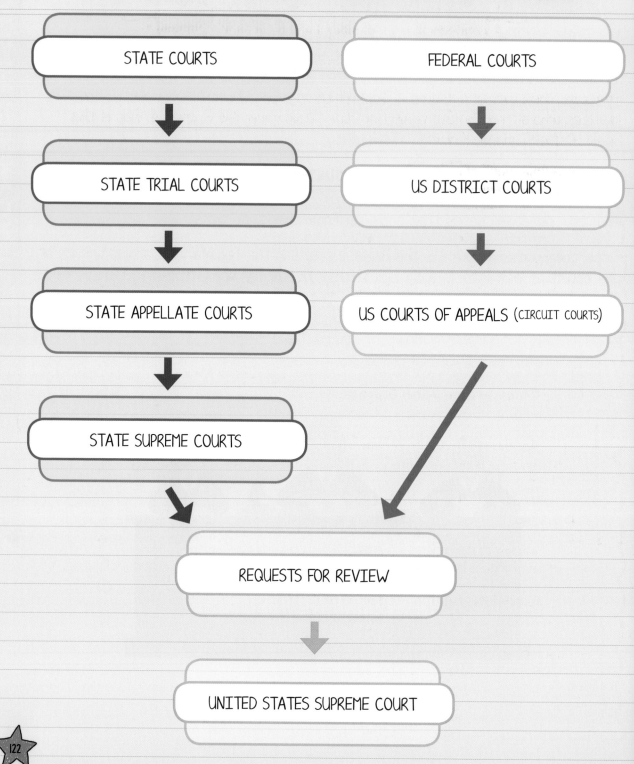

STATE COURTS

FEDERAL COURTS

STATE TRIAL COURTS

US DISTRICT COURTS

STATE APPELLATE COURTS

US COURTS OF APPEALS (CIRCUIT COURTS)

STATE SUPREME COURTS

REQUESTS FOR REVIEW

UNITED STATES SUPREME COURT

WHO ARE THE SUPREME COURT JUSTICES?

Although the number could be changed by Congress, there are currently nine justices who sit on the Supreme Court, including one chief justice, who is the head of the Supreme Court.

Associate Justice Clarence Thomas
(Appointed by George H. W. Bush in 1991)

Associate Justice Ruth Bader Ginsburg
(Appointed by Bill Clinton in 1993)

Associate Justice Stephen G. Breyer
(Appointed by Bill Clinton in 1994)

Chief Justice John G. Roberts, Jr.
(Appointed by George W. Bush in 2005)

Associate Justice Samuel A. Alito
(Appointed by George W. Bush in 2006)

Associate Justice Sonia Sotomayor
(Appointed by Barack Obama in 2009)

Associate Justice Elena Kagan
(Appointed by Barack Obama in 2010)

Associate Justice Neil M. Gorsuch
(Appointed by Donald Trump in 2017)

Associate Justice Brett M. Kavanaugh
(Appointed by Donald Trump in 2018)

Ruth Bader Ginsburg

Justices of the US Supreme Court, November 30, 2018: Seated from left: Associate Justices Stephen Breyer and Clarence Thomas, Chief Justice John Roberts, Associate Justices Ruth Bader Ginsburg and Samuel Alito. Standing from left: Associate Justices Neil Gorsuch, Sonia Sotomayor, Elena Kagan, and Brett Kavanaugh

In 1937, President Franklin Delano Roosevelt threatened to add up to six justices to the Supreme Court so that he could get more favorable rulings on legislation he proposed during his time in office. This was called "court packing." The idea never passed, and the number of Supreme Court justices has remained at nine since 1869.

HOW DO YOU GET ON THE SUPREME COURT?

The Constitution does not have a list of requirements for becoming a member of the Supreme Court as it does for Congress and the presidency. The only quality it mentions is that the judge must exhibit "good behavior." Most of the time, the president is going to nominate a candidate that currently serves on the circuit court of appeals, due to the similar functions of the courts.

Supreme Court justices serve for life. Whenever one of the nine Supreme Court justices retires, dies, or is impeached and removed, the sitting president gets to nominate a replacement. This is one of the biggest responsibilities the president has, as he or she is placing someone on the court who will have an impact on the country for decades beyond their presidency.

SOME OF THE THINGS THAT A PRESIDENT CONSIDERS WHEN SELECTING A NEW SUPREME COURT JUDGE ARE:

EXPERIENCE: Even though it's not required, most nominees have either served in the government or have substantial judicial experience. The majority also have law degrees.

POLITICAL IDEOLOGY: This has become the most important criteria in recent years. Democratic presidents tend to nominate judges with a more liberal viewpoint, while Republican presidents nominate those who are more conservative.

ETHNICITY AND GENDER: The vast majority of Supreme Court justices since the court's creation have been white males (more than 95 percent). Recent presidents have made ethnicity and gender more important factors in the nominating process. Thurgood Marshall, the first African American Supreme Court justice, was appointed by Lyndon B. Johnson in 1967. Sandra Day O'Connor was the first female justice on the Supreme Court; she was appointed by Ronald Reagan in 1981. Both of Barack Obama's appointments were women, including the first Hispanic Supreme Court justice, Sonia Sotomayor.

Once the president has made his or her nomination, the new justice nominee then needs to be approved by the Senate. This process usually takes about two months from nomination to approval. After being nominated, the potential justice meets with members of the Senate informally to discuss their credentials and their views on the role of the Supreme Court. Then the Senate Judiciary Committee questions the nominee in a public forum about their fitness to serve on the highest court in the land. After this, the committee recommends to the rest of the Senate whether they should approve the nomination or reject it.

The Senate needs to confirm the nominee with a majority vote. A majority is often achieved when the Senate is controlled by the same party as the president. When that is the case, the president usually nominates a judge who not only shares a similar ideology, but who might even be a little more partial toward the president's own political party.

The president needs to nominate a different type of nominee when his or her party does not control the majority of the Senate. In those instances, the president usually nominates much more moderate candidates to gain approval from the rival party.

WHO ELSE WORKS AT THE SUPREME COURT?

SUPREME COURT CLERKS: They assist Supreme Court justices by conducting research, recommending which cases to hear, and preparing opinion drafts for their justice.

SOLICITOR GENERAL: This person is sometimes referred to as America's lawyer. He or she is appointed by the president to represent the US government's interests in the Supreme Court. There have been six former solicitors general that have become Supreme Court justices, including current justice Elena Kagan.

PRESIDENT RONALD REAGAN GREETS A YOUNG JOHN ROBERTS DURING A PHOTO OPPORTUNITY IN THE OVAL OFFICE IN 1983.

FACT

Many Supreme Court justices worked as clerks. John Roberts, the current chief justice of the United States, served as a clerk for then-justice William Rehnquist.

127

WHICH CASES DOES IT RULE ON?

Very few cases actually make it to the Supreme Court. The collection of cases that the Supreme Court hears each year is called the **docket**. In a calendar year, more than 7,000 case are appealed to the Supreme Court, but the justices usually only agree to hear between seventy and ninety of them. The cases that end up on the Supreme Court's docket are either from the federal courts of appeals or from the various state supreme courts. Most of these cases involve a state violating a federal law or a citizen who feels his or her constitutional rights have been violated.

For instance, when the state of Florida only provided attorneys to citizens charged with capital crimes, Clarence Gideon represented himself at trial and through the entire appeals process in the Florida courts, eventually losing in the Florida Supreme Court. The US Supreme Court agreed to take his case because Florida was not granting its citizens the constitutional right of the Sixth Amendment. Gideon won his case in the Supreme Court and established the **precedent** that a state cannot prevent a defendant from having legal counsel.

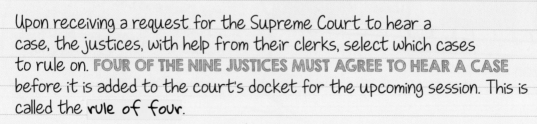

Upon receiving a request for the Supreme Court to hear a case, the justices, with help from their clerks, select which cases to rule on. FOUR OF THE NINE JUSTICES MUST AGREE TO HEAR A CASE before it is added to the court's docket for the upcoming session. This is called the **rule of four**.

The procedure is the same for any case that is accepted by the Supreme Court. First, both sides submit briefs explaining why they believe that they should win the case. A brief is when lawyers argue their case in written form. The justices might also receive briefs from outside parties, usually interest groups that try to convince the court to rule in their favor. The justices and their clerks then read all the briefs before the two parties have their day in court.

On the day the trial begins, each side has thirty minutes to present its oral arguments to try to persuade the justices to rule in their favor. There is very little new information provided to the justices during the trial, because they have read the facts of the case and all the accompanying briefs associated with the case ahead of time. So, the justices spend most of the thirty minutes asking the lawyers to clarify what they wrote in their briefs so they can have a full understanding of the arguments being presented by both sides.

A day or two after the case is heard, the justices meet in a conference where they discuss and debate the case with each other and eventually reach a decision. Each of the nine justices gets to cast a vote. A decision is reached when at least five of the nine justices agree on the verdict.

The official decision of the court is known as the majority opinion. The majority opinion becomes the new precedent for the nation once the decision is published by the court. That means that all fifty states must accept and apply the decision of the Supreme Court. For example, when the court desegregated schools in Brown v. Board of Education, all the states had to integrate their classrooms.

The justices who are in the minority, or the losing side, can write a dissenting opinion where they explain why they disagree with the court's majority opinion. A dissenting opinion might be used in order to influence future judgments in similar cases or situations.

IMPORTANT SUPREME COURT CASES

Only about 1 percent of cases appealed to the Supreme Court are heard by the highest court in the land. Luckily, the courts often use their power to address policies that the other two branches of government can't or won't make decisions on, such as legalizing same-sex marriage, desegregating schools, and ruling on the privacy rights of citizens. These cases can have an enormous impact on the entire country. Here is a list of the few landmark decisions of the Supreme Court over the years.

MARBURY V. MADISON (1803): Established the power of judicial review, which gave the Supreme Court the power to rule on the Constitution.

BROWN V. BOARD OF EDUCATION OF TOPEKA, KANSAS (1954): Desegregated schools by ruling that the practice of "separate but equal" was unconstitutional.

MIRANDA V. ARIZONA (1966): The court found that the Fifth and Sixth Amendments require police to inform individuals in custody that they have a right to remain silent and to be assisted by an attorney.

TINKER V. DES MOINES (1969): Ruled that school children do not lose their freedom of speech rights while in school.

OBERGEFELL V. HODGES (2015): Made same-sex marriage legal in the United States.

wHO ELSE wORKS IN THE GOVERNMENT?

The president, the members of Congress, and the Supreme Court justices all play a crucial role in the United States government. But they can't do it alone. There are a number of other important people within the executive and the legislative branches who assist them in running the country smoothly.

The president's help in the executive branch comes from members of the federal bureaucracy. The bureaucracy is a collection of appointed and non-appointed officials who carry out the laws that are passed by Congress. These officials advise the president or assist him or her on how best to implement new policies.

THE CABINET

One of the president elect's first jobs is to nominate fifteen people for his or her **cabinet**. In addition to serving as an advisory body, the members of the cabinet are also the heads of different executive departments. They oversee these departments and enforce laws in their specific areas. But before a new member of the cabinet can get to work, they first have to be approved by the Senate.

Once the president elect has made nominations for each cabinet department, the Senate meets with the candidates. Senators ask the candidates questions about their history and their qualifications for joining the president's cabinet—sort of like a job interview. Once the reviews are over, the Senate votes on whether or not to confirm the nominees. Unless there is a serious problem with the nominee, most get confirmed.

FACT

Each of the fifteen department heads has the title "secretary," like secretary of defense or secretary of education. The only exception is the head of the Justice Department; this person is called the attorney general.

WHAT ARE THE CABINET DEPARTMENTS?

The cabinet was first created by President George Washington to help him sufficiently carry out government policies. He created three departments: state, treasury, and war (which would later become defense). As the United States has grown, twelve more departments have been added to aid the president in his role as chief executive. Here is a brief summary of the fifteen departments and their roles.

DEPARTMENT OF STATE (1789): Its primary job is to promote American foreign policy (dealing with other countries). The first secretary of state was Thomas Jefferson.

DEPARTMENT OF THE TREASURY (1789): It is responsible for promoting economic prosperity and ensuring the financial security of the United States. The Treasury prints all paper currency and mints all coins. It also collects taxes and makes sure that the government has enough money to keep everything running. Alexander Hamilton was the first secretary of the treasury.

DEPARTMENT OF DEFENSE (1789): This office was originally called the Department of War, but it was renamed in 1947. Its job is to provide the military that defends our country. It is the largest government agency, with more than 2.8 million employees.

DEPARTMENT OF THE INTERIOR (1849): This department is responsible for the protection and management of most federal land and natural resources, including America's national parks and wildlife.

DEPARTMENT OF AGRICULTURE (1862): Known as the USDA, it ensures that our food is safe and properly grown and prepared.

DEPARTMENT OF JUSTICE (1870): This office promotes public safety and enforces the law. The Federal Bureau of Investigation (FBI) is its most well-known agency.

DEPARTMENT OF COMMERCE (1913): This department serves as the voice of businesses. Its main purpose is to create jobs, promote economic growth, encourage development, and block harmful trade practices of other nations.

DEPARTMENT OF LABOR (1913): It makes sure that America's workers are protected by promoting safe working conditions and preventing discrimination in the workplace.

DEPARTMENT OF HOUSING AND URBAN DEVELOPMENT (1965): This office created federal programs to help Americans with their housing needs. It supports community development and increased access to affordable housing free from discrimination.

DEPARTMENT OF TRANSPORTATION (1966): It is responsible for developing and maintaining the nation's highways, roads, rail lines, and airways. Its job is to create the safest and most efficient transportation system in the world.

DEPARTMENT OF ENERGY (1977): This department is concerned with advancing the economic security of America by implementing policies regarding nuclear power, fossil fuels, and alternative energy sources.

DEPARTMENT OF EDUCATION (1980): Its mission is to serve America's students by promoting student achievement and preparing them for global competitiveness.

DEPARTMENT OF HEALTH AND HUMAN SERVICES (1980):
This office was created to protect the health of all Americans and provide essential human services. It encourages healthy habits and helps deal with any disease outbreaks in America.

DEPARTMENT OF VETERANS AFFAIRS (1989):
This department provides healthcare services and benefit programs to former military personnel and their families.

DEPARTMENT OF HOMELAND SECURITY (2002):
This department was founded by President George W. Bush as a result of the attacks on September 11, 2001. Its goal is to secure the nation's citizens within and outside its borders. It prepares and responds to domestic emergencies, especially terrorism.

LEADERSHIP OF CONGRESS

There are more than five hundred members of Congress, so it's only natural that congresspeople compete for power within their respective chambers. Both the Democratic and Republican parties choose leaders who have a great deal of power over the lawmaking process. These leaders are usually the members who have held their seats in the House or Senate for a long time. This collection of elected officials use their leadership positions to make sure that their party speaks with one voice when voting on a bill or commenting on a policy proposal.

LEADERS IN THE HOUSE

SPEAKER OF THE HOUSE

The speaker is the most powerful person in the House. He or she is the leader of the majority party. If the majority party votes together, they can pass or defeat any proposed legislation, so the speaker essentially decides what legislation passes in the House.

WHIP

This is an important position for both the Democrats and the Republicans. This party leader makes sure that all the members of their party are voting the same way on a bill. The whip meets with members who are not planning to vote with their party and tries to convince them to change their minds. Sometimes they do this by offering the party members incentives, such as support on a future bill they propose.

MINORITY LEADER

He or she is the leader of the minority party in the House. The minority leader uses the media and public speeches to try to rally support against the majority party. He or she stands to become the Speaker of the House if their party becomes the majority after the next election.

★ LeaDeRs in THe SenaTe ★

MAJORITY LEADER

Like the Speaker of the House, this is the most powerful person in the Senate. He or she is the leader of the majority party and decides what legislation passes in the chamber.

MINORITY LEADER

He or she is the leader of the minority party in the Senate. The minority leader provides loyal opposition to the majority party. He or she can become the majority leader if their party wins more seats than the other party after the next election.

WHIP

Like the whip in the House, this is an important position for both the Democrats and the Republicans. The whips are responsible for getting everyone from their party to vote the same way on a bill.

PRESIDENT OF THE SENATE

This position is held by the vice president of the United States. His or her only function is to vote in the Senate if there is a tied vote.

CIVIL SERVICE JOBS

When someone says they are a civil service employee, it means that they work for the government.

SOME OF THE JOBS THAT FALL UNDER THE FEDERAL, STATE, OR LOCAL GOVERNMENTS INCLUDE:

- ★ Engineers
- ★ Teachers
- ★ Social workers
- ★ Air traffic controllers
- ★ Judges
- ★ Members of the armed forces

These highly competitive jobs can be obtained in a variety of ways. One could be appointed, elected, or hired if you qualify for one of these positions. Some positions might require a candidate to pass a civil service exam in order to qualify, but most just require applying and having the necessary skills to compete for the position.

DOES THE GOVERNMENT EVER STOP WORKING?

A government shutdown may occur if Congress fails to fund the government: For instance, if the president and Congress or the House and Senate cannot agree on the federal budget. During a government shutdown, the government closes "all nonessential" services, such as national parks and White House tours, while essential services, such as the armed forces, border protection, air traffic controllers, and police and fire departments, all continue to operate.

wHAT CAN I DO?

Learning how the government works is just the first step to becoming—and staying—an active citizen. Even if you aren't eligible to vote just yet, there are still many things you can do to get people involved, raise awareness, and engage in your government at multiple levels.

Voting is one of the most important things you can do as a citizen. It is our civic duty to elect fellow citizens working for the government who will represent our best interests. But don't worry if you're not eighteen yet! Anyone of any age can help others register to vote. This can be very easy because most states now have online registration.

You can also volunteer for a political campaign, even if you can't vote for the candidate yourself. Visit the websites of the candidates you support and sign up through their volunteer forms. (Just make sure that the campaign doesn't have any age restrictions, and that your parents or guardians are okay with you volunteering.) Look for rallies in your area. If you're able to attend, make banners and posters supporting the candidate's ideas to bring along.

You can also help educate fellow citizens by spreading positive information about the candidate you support. From mobilizing voters through phone calls, going door-to-door in your local neighborhood, or even putting a yard sign outside of where you live, there are many ways to spread your candidate's message. And don't forget about social media. You can create hashtags, memes, or GIFs to help raise awareness for your preferred candidates and your favorite causes, or share those that others have created.

Starting with an achievable goal is key. Matt Deitsch, a chief strategist for March For Our Lives (and one of my former students) usually highlights Dr. King's "Letter from Birmingham Jail" when he speaks to students. Dr. King's letter was a powerful statement made through a small protest: The march that led to his arrest had fewer than fifty people. Then Matt asks the students, "Who here thinks they can organize less than fifty people?" This is a great reminder that you don't have to do something big in order to make a big difference.

Martin Luther King, Jr.

One of the best ways to make sure that your legislators are representing you and not interest groups is to **ENGAGE WITH THEM DIRECTLY** and **HOLD THEM ACCOUNTABLE** for their actions. Try to attend any events that your elected officials offer, like town halls, and follow them on social media to see what they are doing and where they will be. If you disagree with something that they support, call their office, write them a postcard, or send them an email. You can find their contact information easily on government websites. You can find scripts or guides on what to say online, too. There are some services that will even send emails to your congresspeople automatically! Social media is another place where you can respectfully hold your elected officials accountable for their actions.

STAY ENGAGED in the political process by paying attention to the news. It's easy to keep updated by following news networks, politicians, and political reporters on social media, by watching political debates, and by researching trending political topics. Social media platforms can be used to spread news, organize, and connect with others who share your ideas. Some activists have even used hashtags to bring people together and start movements.

SPREAD THE WORD about your cause to other people in your community and any local or state officials who might support your idea. The more people who know about what you're trying to do, the better!

PETITIONS can be used to change policies by raising a specific concern so other citizens can become aware of an issue. Create a document stating what you'd like to change and then ask others to sign it, showing their support. When creating a petition, be sure to develop a clear and concise argument about what you are trying to change, and have a goal for how many signatures you want to get.

In October 2019, a group of kids started a petition to close school the day after Halloween. They got more than one million signatures! The size of the petition caused the media to cover the story, and it could result in the closure of schools on November 1st in the future. Like everything else, petitions are much easier to promote today because social media allows you to reach more people at a much faster rate.

CHANGE THE WORLD!

MARCHES AND PROTESTS have been part of the American political process for centuries. The goal of these events is to raise awareness for your cause and ultimately to get legislators to pass laws to benefit your group. Marches and protests are both protected by the First Amendment's freedom of assembly and freedom of petition clauses.

After the tragedy at my high school, Marjory Stoneman Douglas High School, our students organized the March For Our Lives, the largest student-led march in American history, in just over a month, with the goal to end senseless gun violence.

MOMENTS AND MOVEMENTS:

December 16, 1773:
During the Boston Tea Party, American colonists dress up as Native Americans and dump tea from the East India Company into Boston Harbor to protest the Tea Act. Only a few years later, the colonists declare independence.

July 19-20, 1848:
The Seneca Falls Convention is held in upstate New York to discuss the end of discrimination against women. The event, organized by Elizabeth Cady Stanton and Lucretia Mott, is attended by approximately 300 women.

1760	1780	1800	1850	1860

January 1, 1863:
Abraham Lincoln signs the Emancipation Proclamation, which says that all enslaved people within the rebelling Confederate states are free. Although the proclamation does not actually free anyone, it helps shape the Civil War's goal of ending slavery in the United States.

August 1786-June 1787:
Daniel Shays leads a farmers' rebellion in Massachusetts protesting high taxes. Shays' Rebellion proves just how ineffective the Articles of Confederation are, and the protest leads to the Articles being replaced with the US Constitution.

A TIMELINE OF PROGRESS

September 1919–January 1920:
More than 350,000 steel workers go on strike in Pittsburgh, Pennsylvania, to protest low wages, long hours, and poor working conditions. The strike causes more than half of the United States steel industry to shut down.

December 6, 1865:
The Thirteenth Amendment is added to the Constitution, abolishing slavery.

August 18, 1920:
The Nineteenth Amendment is ratified, giving women the right to vote.

1870   1900   1920   1930

(continued)

March 3, 1913:
The first women's suffrage parade is held in Washington, DC, the day before Woodrow Wilson's inauguration. The event is organized by Alice Paul and attended by more than 8,000 marchers.

December 10, 1924:
Henry Gerber founds the Society of Human Rights, the first documented American gay rights organization, in Chicago.

August 14, 1935:
The Social Security Act is passed, which establishes a program of permanent federal assistance to people with disabilities and the elderly, among others.

June 14, 1938:
The Fair Labor Standards Act is passed, requiring a minimum age of employment and regulates working hours for children by law.

December 1, 1955:
Rosa Parks is arrested for civil disobedience for refusing to give up her seat on a public bus in Montgomery, Alabama. This leads to the year-long Montgomery Bus Boycott (December 5, 1955–December 20, 1956) and the ruling that segregation on buses is unconstitutional.

1935   1940   1950   1960

Jan 10-11, 1957: Civil rights leaders meet in Atlanta and form the Southern Christian Leadership Conference (SCLC), with the goal of coordinating nonviolent protests against segregation and racial discrimination. Martin Luther King, Jr. is chosen as its first president. The SCLC organizes voter registration drives, sit-ins, and a four-month campaign in Birmingham, Alabama.

September 27, 1962: Rachel Carson publishes *Silent Spring*, a book about the dangers of using pesticides. Her book launches the early environmental movement in the United States, which results in the creation of the Environmental Protection Agency in 1970.

September 25, 1957:
The Little Rock Nine attend their first full day at Central High School in Arkansas, after three weeks of the National Guard preventing them from entering the building. They are the first group of African American students to integrate a public high school.

August 28, 1963:
Approximately 250,000 people participate in the March on Washington to draw attention to the continuing struggles of African Americans. At the end of the march, Martin Luther King, Jr. gives his renowned "I Have a Dream" speech in front of the Lincoln Memorial.

July 2, 1964:
The Civil Rights Act of 1964 is signed by President Lyndon B. Johnson. Among other issues, the law prevents employment discrimination due to race, sex, religion, or national origin.

October 21, 1967:
More than 100,000 protesters gather at the Lincoln Memorial to protest the long and costly Vietnam War (1954–1973), ending in a riot at the Pentagon.

1965

1970

(continued)

June 28, 1969:
The Stonewall Riots, a six-day protest, begin after police raid and mistreat patrons in a gay bar in New York City. The riots spark the beginning of the gay rights movement in the United States. Exactly one year later, the first gay pride parade occurs in New York City.

April 22, 1970:
More than 20 million American citizens take part in the first Earth Day, encouraging environmental protection.

November 1969–June 1971:
The American Indian Movement (AIM), working with several tribes, occupies the closed Alcatraz Federal Penitentiary to protest police brutality, poverty, and overall mistreatment of Native Americans in the United States.

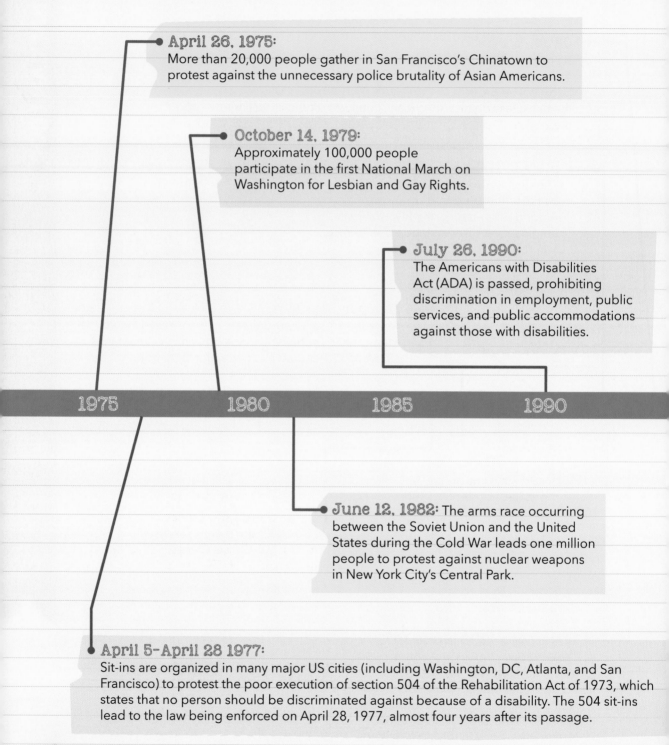

April 26, 1975:
More than 20,000 people gather in San Francisco's Chinatown to protest against the unnecessary police brutality of Asian Americans.

October 14, 1979:
Approximately 100,000 people participate in the first National March on Washington for Lesbian and Gay Rights.

July 26, 1990:
The Americans with Disabilities Act (ADA) is passed, prohibiting discrimination in employment, public services, and public accommodations against those with disabilities.

1975   1980   1985   1990

June 12, 1982: The arms race occurring between the Soviet Union and the United States during the Cold War leads one million people to protest against nuclear weapons in New York City's Central Park.

April 5-April 28 1977:
Sit-ins are organized in many major US cities (including Washington, DC, Atlanta, and San Francisco) to protest the poor execution of section 504 of the Rehabilitation Act of 1973, which states that no person should be discriminated against because of a disability. The 504 sit-ins lead to the law being enforced on April 28, 1977, almost four years after its passage.

July 13, 2013:
Black Lives Matter is founded by African American activists to fight against violence and racism toward black people. The group continues to hold marches protesting the senseless deaths of African Americans at the hands of the police.

January 21, 2017:
The Women's March becomes the largest single-day demonstration in US history. More than 3.5 million people participate in the protest for gender equality and civil rights in the United States, with hundreds of thousands more participating across the globe.

2010   2015   2020

June 26, 2015:
The United States Supreme Court legalizes same-sex marriage.

September 20-27, 2019:
Over four million people participate in more than 4,000 different marches across 150 countries for the Global Climate Strike, led by sixteen-year-old Greta Thunberg from Sweden.

March 24, 2018:
An estimated one million people across the country attend the March For Our Lives, a student-led demonstration in support of legislation to prevent gun violence in the United States.

CONCLUSION

The world has never been more complicated than it is right now. But it's also never been easier to stay connected, to get involved, and to make a difference. I hope this book has taught you how our great democracy started, how it works, and how we can all play a big part in making it work for us.

There are so many ways that you can improve our country and our world. Remember to stay informed about what is going on in your community. Find something that you are passionate about and immerse yourself in it. Set achievable goals and create a clear plan to

accomplish them. The amount of information that you can gather is endless; the more you know, the more you will understand and the more you will be able to contribute to your cause.

Don't forget to ask your friends, family, and teachers to help you along the way. Strive to become an expert in the things that matter most to you. Then let others know about your passion. Spread your message and frame your argument—whether through social media or a face-to-face conversation. Reach out to your elected officials and know what they believe in. And if you don't like what they are doing, then petition, march, rally, and support their future opponents.

Our government and our democracy is a living, changing thing. In order to pledge our allegiance to our country, we need to trust that our leaders are standing up for us, just like we're standing up for them.

When you are old enough, make sure you register to vote. Then use that power to support candidates and policies that reflect your views. Until then, make sure the adults in your life are participating in the political process. There are many ways that they can help you and also make changes of their own.

I will continue to try to inspire all those that I come into contact with in the hope that they find and follow their passion — whether it's something as small as switching to reusable straws or as big as traveling the country rallying support for tangible changes to gun laws.

We live in a great country that allows every person to effect change. There are new issues popping up every day. How we deal with these new problems is what is going to define the next generation— your generation. Don't be a bystander. Be a problem solver.

 ARE YOU READY TO BE
THE NEXT GREAT CHANGEMAKER?

GLOSSARY

ABSENTEE BALLOT
A way of voting that is completed in advance by a voter who is unable to be at the polls on Election Day.

ABSOLUTE MONARCHY
A form of government in which a monarch (like a king or queen) has unlimited power and makes all governmental decisions for the country.

ADJOURN
To close or end a government meeting or court session.

AMEND
To change a legal document or law.

AMENDMENT
A change that is made to a legal document or law.

APPEAL
To ask for a decision made by a court of law to be changed.

APPOINT
To choose someone for a job.

AUTHORITARIAN
A government in which citizens have very few freedoms and opportunities to participate in governmental decision-making.

BICAMERAL

A legislature with two chambers or branches.

BILL

A written plan for a new law that will be debated in Congress.

BOYCOTT

To refuse to take part in something as a way of protesting.

BRIEF

An argument made by a lawyer in written form instead of in person.

BULLY PULPIT

The president's use of all forms of communication to try to persuade the public to support his or her ideas.

CABINET

A committee of advisors responsible for helping the president create government policy.

CAMPAIGN CONTRIBUTION

Money given to political candidates by individuals or groups who support their ideas.

CAUCUS

A meeting at which local members of a political party discuss their preference among the candidates running for office or select representatives to attend a convention.

CENSUS
The official count of the number of people living in a country or district.

CHAIR
The leader of a congressional committee.

CHIEF JUSTICE
The lead judge of the Supreme Court, the chief justice presides over the court in public sessions and private conferences.

CLOTURE
A motion to bring debate to an end and take a vote on a measure or bill.

COMMUNIST
A government in which wealth is shared. A communist government owns things like land, factories, and machinery, and provides its citizens with necessities like food, housing, and clothing.

CONFIRM
To accept someone for a job or position.

CONSENT
Permission to do something, or an agreement to do something.

CONSTITUENT
A voter represented by an elected official.

CONSTITUTIONAL MONARCHY
A form of government in which a monarch serves in a ceremonial role while the government is run by elected officials.

CONVENTION
A large gathering of people who have the same interests, such as a political meeting.

DELEGATE
Someone who represents their state at a political party convention.

DEMOCRACY
A form of government in which the people choose their leaders in elections.

DICTATORSHIP
An authoritarian form of government in which a single leader or group of leaders has complete control and authority over all decisions made by the government.

DIRECT DEMOCRACY
A democracy in which every person contributes to every decision made by the government.

DISSENTING OPINION
A written explanation as to why the losing side in a court case disagrees with the court's majority decision.

DISTRICT
An area or region that an elected official represents.

DOCKET

The collection of cases that the Supreme Court hears each year.

ELECTOR

A voter chosen to represent a state in the Electoral College system.

ELECTORAL COLLEGE

A system for choosing the president of the United States. Electors cast all of their state's electoral votes for the presidential candidate who receives the most votes from the people of that state.

EXECUTIVE ORDER

The president's power to change the way an executive agency applies a law.

EXECUTIVE PRIVILEGE

The president's ability to keep national security secrets from the public.

EXTRADITION

The action of returning a fugitive who has been charged with or convicted of a crime back to the state (or country) from which they fled.

FASCIST

An authoritarian form of government in which a centralized government is led by an anti-democracy dictator.

FEDERAL BUREAUCRACY

A collection of appointed and non-appointed officials that carry out the laws passed by Congress.

FEDERALISM
A system of government in which the national and state governments share power over the people.

FILIBUSTER
A tactic in Congress of continuing to talk about a bill in order to delay or prevent a vote on the bill from occurring.

FIRST GENTLEMAN
The title given to an official White House host should the president's spouse or partner be male.

FIRST LADY
The title held by the official hostess of the White House. Historically, this role has been filled by the wife of the president of the United States.

FOREIGN POLICY
A government's plan or principle for dealing with and making decisions regarding other countries.

GERRYMANDER
To change the boundaries of a voting district to favor one political party or group.

INAUGURATION
The ceremony of swearing in a public official.

INCUMBENT
A person currently in a position or office.

IMPEACH

To bring formal charges against a public official who may have committed a crime or other illegal acts while in office.

INTEREST GROUP

A group of people who share a common goal about how laws should be written.

JOINT COMMITTEE

A committee made up of members of both the House and the Senate that is formed to bring attention to a larger issue. Joint committees are often used for investigative purposes.

JOINT CONFERENCE COMMITTEE

A type of joint committee formed after a proposed bill has passed in both chambers, tasked with figuring out how to balance the House's version of the bill with the Senate's.

JOINT SESSION

A session of Congress at the beginning of each calendar year when all 100 Senators and 435 House members gather together.

JUSTICE

A judge who hears cases in a court of law.

LAME-DUCK PERIOD

The time period between a presidential election and the new president being sworn into office.

LITIGATION
Use of the court system to stop or defend policies based on an advocacy group's interests.

LOBBYING
The practice of providing specific information to lawmakers and other elected officials about the possible effects of proposed legislation.

MAJORITY OPINION
A judicial opinion agreed to by more than half of the members of a court.

MAJORITY PARTY
The political party in Congress that holds more than half of the total number of seats.

MASS MOBILIZATION
A large gathering of people intending to raise awareness for a cause and to change policy to benefit the group or cause.

MINORITY PARTY
The political party in Congress that holds fewer than half of the total number of seats.

MONARCHY
A form of government with a king or queen as its head of government.

NOMINATE
To propose that someone would be the right person to do a job.

NOMINATION
An official recommendation of someone for a position or office.

ORDER OF SUCCESSION
An ordered list of people who would take over the president's job if he or she should die, resign, or be removed from office during his or her term.

PARDON
To forgive or excuse someone legally or officially, or to release the person from punishment.

PLURALITY
A circumstance where one candidate receives more votes than any other candidate.

POCKET VETO
An indirect veto of a legislative bill that occurs when the president or a governor refuses to sign the bill until it is too late for it to be dealt with during the legislative session.

POLL NUMBER
The results of a canvassing of randomly selected people to gather information and opinions about a topic, such as a preferred political candidate.

POPULAR VOTE
The choice expressed by the votes cast by the citizens in a district, state, or country.

POPULOUS
Having a large population.

PRECEDENT
Something done, said, or written that becomes an example to be followed in the future.

PRESIDENT ELECT
A person who has won the election for president but has not yet been sworn into office.

PRIMARY
An election to choose a party candidate who will run in the general election.

RATIFY
To agree to or approve officially.

REBUTTAL
A speech that presents the other side of an issue or argument.

REPRESENTATIVE DEMOCRACY
A form of government in which citizens choose others to represent them through elections. These representatives then make decisions for the government.

REPUBLIC
A form of government in which citizens elect other people to represent them in the government's decision making.

RIDER
An addition to a bill that is not directly related to that bill.

RULE OF FOUR
The rule that four of the nine Supreme Court justices must agree to hear a case before it is added to the court's docket.

SELECT COMMITTEE
A temporary committee (also called a special committee) created to deal with a specific issue not covered by any standing committee. Select committees are often formed to carry out investigations.

SENIOR
Someone who has been a member of a committee longer than other committee members.

SOCIALISM
A government in which there is very little private property and the government provides most things for its citizens.

SOVEREIGNTY
The authority of a state to govern itself.

STANDING COMMITTEE
A permanent congressional committee. This is where a bill is changed and amended until it is ready for the full chamber to vote on it.

SUFFRAGE
The right to vote.

TREASON
The crime of betraying one's country by spying for another country or by helping an enemy during a war.

UNCONSTITUTIONAL
Not keeping with the basic principles or laws set forth in the constitution of a state or country, especially the Constitution of the United States.

UNCONTESTED
A decision that is not being disputed or challenged.

UNICAMERAL
A legislature with a single chamber.

VETO
The right or power of a president or governor to reject a bill that has been passed by legislature to prevent it from becoming a law.

INDEX

Note: Page numbers in italics refer to photographs and illustrations.